# Law, Psychiatry
## and the
# Mentally Disordered Offender

# Law, Psychiatry and the Mentally Disordered Offender

## Volume I

*Edited by*

**LYNN M. IRVINE, JR., C.S.W., A.C.S.W.**
*Mental Health Administrator*
*Department of Mental Health*
*Illinois Security Hospital*
*Chester, Illinois*

*and*

**TERRY B. BRELJE, Ph.D.**
*Administrator*
*Department of Corrections*
*Psychiatric Division*
*Menard, Illinois*

**CHARLES C THOMAS · PUBLISHER**
*Springfield · Illinois · U.S.A.*

*Published and Distributed Throughout the World by*
CHARLES C THOMAS · PUBLISHER
BANNERSTONE HOUSE
301-327 East Lawrence Avenue, Springfield, Illinois, U.S.A.

© *1972, by* CHARLES C THOMAS · PUBLISHER
ISBN 0-398-02530-4
Library of Congress Catalog Card Number: 72-75921

*With* THOMAS BOOKS *careful attention is given to all details of
manufacturing and design. It is the Publisher's desire to present books
that are satisfactory as to their physical qualities and artistic possibilities
and appropriate for their particular use.* THOMAS BOOKS *will be true
to those laws of quality that assure a good name and good will.*

Proceedings from an Institute held on
November 17, 18, and 19, 1970 at
Southern Illinois University, Carbondale, Illinois

*Printed in the United States of America*
*J-2*

*To*

*The Mentally Disordered Offender*

# CONTRIBUTORS

## MARVIN CHAPMAN, M.D.
*Administrator, Wisconsin Sex Crimes Law Programs*
*Clinical Director*
*Central State Hospital*
*Waupun, Wisconsin*

## P. J. CICCONE, M.D.
*Director*
*United States Medical Center*
*Springfield, Missouri*

## J. C. FOLSOM, M.D.
*Hospital Director*
*Veterans Administration Hospital*
*Tuscaloosa, Alabama*

## LEO E. HOLLISTER, M.D.
*Associate Chief of Staff*
*Veterans Administration Hospital*
*Palo Alto, California*

## LEONARD HORECKER, M.D.
*Staff Psychiatrist*
*Illinois Security Hospital*
*Chester, Illinois*

## ROGER S. KIGER, M.D.
*Chief of Forensic Psychiatry*
*Director of Maximum Security Unit*
*Utah State Hospital*
*Provo, Utah*

## NORVAL MORRIS, Ph.D.
*Director*
*Center for the Study of Criminal Justice*
*University of Chicago*
*Chicago, Illinois*

**JONAS R. RAPPEPORT, M.D.**

*Chief Medical Officer*
*Medical Service of the Supreme Bench of Baltimore*
*Baltimore, Maryland*

**RUSSELL SETTLE, SR., M.D.**

*Menninger Foundation*
*Topeka, Kansas*

**WERNER TUTEUR, M.D.**

*Clinical Director and Forensic Psychiatrist*
*Elgin State Hospital*
*Elgin, Illinois*

**LEONARD ZUNIN, M.D.**

*Director*
*Glasser Institute of Reality Therapy*
*Los Angeles, California*

*Speech is civilization itself. The word, even the most contradictory word, preserves contact — it is silence which isolates.*

—THOMAS MANN

# INTRODUCTION

THE EDITORS had the privilege of being part of an active effort to upgrade the treatment programs for the mentally disordered offender in the State of Illinois. During that process, it became apparent that there was very little data available on which to rely. In an attempt to alleviate this situation, the editors began formulating plans to bring together a large number of individuals who were similarly involved. The Institute on Law, Psychiatry, and the Mentally Disordered Offender was the result of that effort. It is our hope that the papers will be beneficial in all efforts to provide more effective, responsible, and humane care and treatment for the mentally disordered offender.

# ACKNOWLEDGMENTS

MANY WERE INVOLVED in the planning, organization, and operation of the Institute. Those singled out for special recognition for their encouragement, assistance, and support follow:

Extension and Adult Education
Southern Illinois University
Carbondale
Andrew H. Marcec
Carole Vogt

*Foundation*
W. Clement & Jessie V. Stone Foundation

*Pharmaceutical Houses*
Geigy Pharmaceuticals
Hoffman-LaRoche Incorporated
Pfizer Pharmaceuticals
Pfizer Laboratories Division
J. B. Rocrig Division
Sandoz Pharmaceuticals
Schering Corporation
Smith, Kline, & French Laboratories

*Publishers*
Aldine Publishing Company
Charles C Thomas, Publisher
John Wiley & Sons, Inc.
The University of Chicago Press
The University of Michigan Press

*Individuals*

Ralph H. Albers          Martha E. Brelje
Everett R. Beck          Matthew T. Brelje

[xiii]

Mark Brosche
Terry Carlton
Michael R. Clowers
Betty E. Derickson
Frank E. Derickson
Marian W. Greager
Ralph W. Hay
Alice W. Irvine
Jane W. Irvine
Sally G. Irvine
David L. Jewell
Donald M. Jungewaelter
Geneva Killion

William D. Lodge
Rosemary Mahan
Betty M. Moore
Bonnie Phillips
Martha Roberts
Albert F. Scheckenbach
Earl J. Schnoeker
Robert C. Steck, M.D.
Jack Thomas
Vernon J. Uffelman
William Vollmer
Betty Wagner

L.M.I. AND T.B.B.

# CONTENTS

# Law, Psychiatry
## and the
## Mentally Disordered Offender

## Chapter 1

# THE CRIMINAL JUSTICE SYSTEM AND PSYCHIATRY PAST, PRESENT, AND FUTURE

NORVAL MORRIS

Doctor Morris is one of the most productive and influential legal scholars in America today. His concern about our criminal justice system and the influence he has exerted within that system are well documented. He is, therefore, particularly qualified to address himself to some of the issues that concern both psychiatry and the criminal justice system. His paper outlines those areas which he believes are relevant today and presents some suggestions as to how they might be handled expeditiously. His perception of the need for change and his proposed solutions to the problem are stimulating and provocative. The reader is challenged to work actively toward improving our criminal justice system.

EDITORS

THE TASK OF ADDRESSING a topic entitled "The Criminal Justice System and Psychiatry: Past, Present, and Future" is certainly not confining. The title sets one free; it is hard to think of anything that would not be relevant! It allows a broad sweep, congenial to scholarly superficiality, and no doubt that is what it will attract. Topics like this also reflect, however, the increasing community concern with problems of crime and its control. At last, people have come to recognize that crime does indeed influence where they live, how they live, the quality of life in this country; they recognize that crime problems are set deep in political conflicts and, more particularly, in racial strife. And I hope that this increased interest means that people will no longer tolerate the sheer squalor and inefficiency of our present criminal justice system.

Is it valid to refer to a "criminal justice system"? Is it a system at all? Do police and courts and corrections interrelate into a system

[3]

in which you, the mental health specialists, can relate? I fear the truth is that there is such a lack of planned interfaces between the various agencies involved in the prevention and control of crime and delinquency that it can be described only as a rather ill-defined, inefficient system. I would like to take some time to develop that view.

The criminal justice system has respectable progenitors—a good inheritance, but it is now totally swamped by the flood of business on its inadequate resources. It was a system reasonably well adjusted to the crime control needs of a rural village society; it is proving to be largely incompetent to handle the burgeoning problems of the great cities and the sprawling megalopolis. And despite the pressures upon it, the American criminal justice system continues to be charac-terized by an extraordinary overreach—it seeks to influence more aspects of human behavior than is sought by any other country. Yet, there is very little evidence that the criminal justice system can stop a man going to hell in his own way, and I think that it should not try. Other agencies of government are more attuned to these salva-tion purposes than is the criminal law. I doubt that the criminal law will stop the public drunk from drinking himself to death if he wishes. I doubt that the criminal law will stop people from gambling. I doubt that America's highly moralistic statute book, insofar as sexual behavior is concerned, has made Americans either more or less virtuous than people of similar economic and industrial develop-ment in other countries. It seems to me that there is the same mix of saints and sinners here as elsewhere. And when you contemplate the way in which the statute book seeks to control vagrant, often geriatric behavior, the matter moves to the ludicrous.

All of these laws attempting to control victimless crime have col-lateral disadvantages—quite apart from their ineffectiveness. They tend to be corruptive. It is difficult to keep a vice squad honest any-where in the world. When we use the criminal law to prohibit goods and services which people seem to insist upon purchasing, the prices go up, less attractive vendors push out the more decent vendors, and purchasers are pressed to crime to obtain the commodity or the service—as witness heroin in New York. You and I pay the costs in increased muggings, burglaries, and robberies; and all this without any evidence that the consumption of the prohibited goods or the use of the prohibited services has reduced.

These moralistic, prohibitory laws tend to be racially discriminatory. Take, for example, gambling arrests last year in America. I state them as rates per hundred thousand. Black arrests were 24.86 times as high as white arrests. Now, it may be that blacks gamble more than whites; indeed, poverty is often associated with excessive gambling. But I am confident that blacks do not gamble 25 times as much as whites. The truth is that these types of criminal sanctions are not invoked against categories of behavior per se, but rather against that type of behavior when engaged in by certain social groups. And again we are without any evidence that they are effective.

These victimless crimes distract the criminal law from its proper role. What matters to me, and I suspect to you, is violence to the person, the threat of violence to the person, major deprivations to property, and serious interferences with governmental processes. These are what a decent criminal law is and should be about. Well, is it? Here are the figures: Last year there were approximately six million arrests in America. Three million of these were for "victimless" crimes. Half of all our arrests were for crimes in which nobody identified himself as a victim and said, "criminal law protect me." This vast allocation of criminal law resources to victimless crimes might be excusable if the rest of our system were efficient; but it clearly is not. Let me consider a few highpoints of that inefficiency.

We have over forty thousand independent federal, state, and local police forces. They are of an astonishing diversity; some have reasonably good training programs, some put the policeman in a car with a gun the day he is recruited—and I do not exaggerate. A leading defect in our police forces is that there is no lateral entry. That is to say, if you do very well as a police sergeant in New York City, you cannot transfer to a position of police sergeant in Chicago. Make a comparison with the university; consider a university where the only recruitment would be at the level of assistant lecturer and president of the university. Well, that is common to all our police forces but there is very little else that is common to them. Turn to the courts: We have a most complex system of interlocking jurisdiction of courts, but the bulk of the criminal work is done by the city courts of first instance, and they exemplify the most serious squalor in the system. To my view, speaking as a lawyer concerned in this area, the major deficiencies in the criminal justice system, worse than the jails, worse even than anything in the police or in corrections, is the inefficiency, delay, and sometimes corruption in our city courts of first instance. It is astonishing that this country, built so heavily on law, tolerates such major political patronage and such inefficiency in its judicial system at this level. Furthermore, when one turns from the police and the courts to corrections, one still faces substantial desolation, a system struggling with inadequate resources to deal with burgeoning problems.

How does the criminal justice system process people? Let us look at the flow utilizing the figures published by the National Commission on Violence and concentrate on index crimes, the more serious crimes. Draw in your mind five concentric circles. The outer circle will be index crimes committed; let them number one hundred. How many of these are reported and recorded by the police? We have some reasonably hard evidence on this. The figure is fifty. So let the second inner circle represent the half of index crimes that are reported and recorded. The third inner circle: How many arrests? Twelve. The fourth inner circle: How many convictions of anything at all, not necessarily what they have done? Six. And finally the inner circle: The number of people sentenced to prison or jail? One point five! Now I am no enthusiastic supporter of jails and prisons, but we are dealing with the major crimes, including recidivist crimes, and we have a system in which one hundred serious crimes committed reduces itself to one point five people sentenced to our major sanction. That is an inefficient system. Indeed, the leading characteristic of the American criminal justice system is not its severity but rather its inefficiency, its operative leniency. Our leading technique of disposing of cases remains private enterprise negotiation, plea-bargaining for agreed settlements. We justify this as we justify so much else in the system, by expediency.

So, if I now offer some critical comments about the role of psychiatry in the criminal justice system, you will not think of me as a one-eyed lawyer, conscious of the defects of other professions but not of his own. The psychiatrist is misused in the criminal justice system; he is not involved in the real work; he is kept for gate keeping and for name calling; for diagnosis rather than for treatment—and rarely is anything built upon the diagnosis. Further, the psychiatrist is used to affect a dangerous mixture of the state's police power and the state's mental health power. It seems to me that almost invariably when these two powers are mixed or confused—and I shall try to illustrate this later—injustice and inefficiency must follow. The path of wisdom is to preserve a rigid severance between them. The police power of the state and the mental health power of the state seem to me sufficient unto themselves, functioning separately, to control the upper limits of power that we take over citizens thought to be dangerous. When the problem poses a combination of crime and mental illness, we should not mix the two powers together as we do so frequently. Let me try to develop these prejudices in relation to four areas of relationship between the criminal law and the work of the psychiatrist: (1) the defense of insanity; (2) incompetency to stand trial; (3) the problem of the prediction of dangerousness; and (4) the problem of the psychiatrist's role in the treatment of mentally disturbed criminals. Dealing with four such large topics, I can only make a few points about each, but I am assured that this is the function of a keynote speaker.

## THE DEFENSE OF INSANITY

This topic has turned out, in modern terminology, to be the "copout" in the law-psychiatry dialogue. There are libraries of discussions on the appropriate rules for a defense of insanity to a criminal charge; there are serious discussions of questions like, "How ill must a man be before he is not responsible for his actions?" "What does it mean to say that a man is irresponsible in the eyes of the criminal law?" We rarely lift our eyes from these fascinating philosophic inexactitudes to observe what is actually happening in the criminal courts, prisons, and jails. Let me make a curt submission to you: There should be no defense of insanity to a criminal charge. The accused's mental condition should be relevant to the question whether he did or did not at the time of the act have the prohibited intent with which he is charged. If he is charged with an act done or with the intent to kill, the question of his mental state is relevant only to whether he did or did not at the time have that intent, be it a sane or insane intent. There should be no special rules like McNaughten or Durham.

The defense of insanity being abrogated, evidence of mental illness would be admissible on the intent issue in exactly the same limited way that, for example, deafness, blindness, a heart condition, stomach cramps, illiteracy, stupidity, lack of education, foreignness, drunkenness, and drug addiction are all now admissible—and, of course, I have picked human conditions which have been litigated as relevant to the intent in issue. You must not think that I have offered any particularly new thought; it may be revolutionary, but it is not original. Some of the major commentators on the criminal law have offered that same suggestion, in one or another form. The most sophisticated submission was done by H. L. A. Hart, Professor of Jurisprudence at Oxford; Chief Justice Weintraub of New Jersey has taken a similar view and Dr. Seymour Halleck of Wisconsin likewise. Let me offer just a few points in favor of such a change.

Historically, the defense of insanity made good sense. It operated in capital cases as a way of avoiding the hangman or the fryman, and I'm all in favor of doing that. But that is not the contemporary problem. We are not executing murderers in America nowadays.

How does the defense now operate as a statistical matter? Well, the defense of insanity is pleaded in about 2 percent of criminal cases which come to jury trial. Overwhelmingly, of course, criminal cases are disposed of by pleas or by bench trial; only a very small proportion come to jury trial, and of that small proportion the defense of insanity is pleaded in two in a hundred cases. Almost exclusively, these are cases of murder. Now, I do not think that anyone can visit a local court or a local prison and accept that the frequency of the insanity plea accurately reflects the incidences of the relationship between mental illness and crime. In short, the defense of insanity is pleaded in only a very few notorious cases. It serves newspapers rather than the community. It is largely an irrelevance in the relationship between mental illness and crime. Observe what happens as we "improve" the defense of insanity. The *Durham Rules* were followed within a month in the District of Columbia by a change in the law, making the commitment of a defendant who had successfully pleaded the defense compulsory rather than discretionary as it has been before. The same is true of the American Law Institute's *Model Penal Code* as it is accepted. It is a strange benevolence we are extending; a strange humanism.

Should there not be a defense of living in a black ghetto, if there is a defense of insanity? Now I am not suggesting that there *should* be a defense of living in a ghetto, but I am saying that I do not understand the moral or philosophical differences between the two. Adverse subcultural backgrounds are statistically much more correlated with crime than is psychosis. And it seems to be quite clear that in all but a very few cases adverse social circumstances just as severely circumscribe one's freedom of choice, which a nondeterministic criminal law attributes to the accused person—and every criminal justice system must be nondeterministic.

As George Bernard Shaw said, "Vengence is mine, saith the Lord, which means it is not the Lord Chief Justice's." There are indeed moral differences of guilt between people, but that does not mean that we are capable of measuring those differences or that we should undertake the measurement.

In short, I am submitting that the defense of insanity distracts from the real world. It is used to avoid the problems of psychopathology and crime. The time has come when we should cease wasting our time with it. No self-respecting psychiatrist should let himself be lured into involving himself in such a case.

## COMPETENCE TO STAND TRIAL

The problem of incompetence to stand trial or unfitness to plead turns out, in my view, to be a more difficult issue than the defense of insanity. The law asks: Is the accused fit to advise his counsel, to act the role of an accused? Does he know what the charge is? Is he present in court? Well, in a real sense, nobody is fit for trial except the very hardened, experienced criminal; it is a disturbing process indeed.

With my friend and colleague, Jerome Goldberg, I worked for many months on a committee to refashion our Illinois law relating to competence to stand trial. I think we made some substantial improvements which are in process of legislative acceptance. We have tried to phrase more realistic questions for the psychiatrist, and we have more clearly distinguished the police power from the mental health power so that there is not an immediate assumption that those who are unfit for trial necessarily must be locked up. Having done all that work, I fear that I am gradually coming to the view that in this issue, just as in the defense of insanity, we are facing a non-issue. I think that what we have recommended is wrong; that it was a useful improvement but fundamentally wrong.

The work of Dr. Louis McGarry in Massachusetts is of great importance to those who are interested in this problem. He visited hospitals holding those who had been found incompetent to stand trial, and he found that many could be returned to court for trial. Many of them wanted to go to trial, many were released via trial, and many were acquitted. Many did not need to be locked up; it was a cruel waste of their time, serving no social purpose. He found that if left in such an institution for two years or more, it was very doubtful that anything useful could be done for or with them. Our benevolence in deciding that they were not fit for trial turned out to be not at all benevolent in operation.

Sometimes, I think it is necessary for us to find out if the accused actually committed the criminal act even if he is seriously psychologically disturbed. Also, and by contrast, there are cases on the books of people who are deeply psychologically troubled and not particularly good at playing the role of accused persons whose counsel suspect that they have not at all done the crime with which they are charged, and the counsel wants to test that issue. At times, the state may desire to bring an accused to trial, and he may wish to go to trial even though, whatever our tests, he is clearly incompetent. We should make special rules of court for such situations.

Further, it must be remembered, there is no legal obligation to prosecute an accused person. The power of the prosecutor to enter a *nolle prosequi* is largely unfettered. There is no reason at all why the prosecutor should not include his knowledge of the mental illness of the accused in the exercise of his discretion whether to prosecute or not. But, if the prosecutor thinks the matter worth taking to trial, I doubt very much that mental illness should ever be a ground for precluding trial. I think it should be a ground for limited delay but not for complete preclusion.

It seems to me that we pose the wrong question by asking, "Is this man now fit for trial?" I think the proper question is, "Doctor, if we give you six months to treat this man in the way that you say he needs treatment, either in an institution or in the community, do you

think he will be substantially *more* fit for trial than he is now?"
If there is persuasive evidence in the affirmative in answer to
that question, a continuance should be allowed. If progress is made,
we might be prepared to extend such continuances for a maximum
period of one year. But that should be the outer limit of deferment
for facing this issue of trial. At that time we had better make up
our minds whether or not we are going to try the accused, whatever
his mental illness. It must not be forgotten that if he be civilly com-
mittable, *that* is an entirely proper course to follow, given the present
state of the law. What we should not do is forge the mental health
power and the police power into an instrument of tyranny.

## Defining and Predicting Dangerousness

Psychiatrists frequently offer predictions of dangerousness to the
courts, though they have not done the hard statistical work on which,
alone, valid predictions of dangerousness could be based. Individual
clinical predictions of dangerousness are, in my view, generally of
little value unless they describe the repetition of a given individual's
firmly established behavioral patterns. Predictions other than that
type must be based on categories of statistically established behaviors.
Let me make a comparison with weather prediction. I flew down
here to this meeting, and to the aviator—even to such a poor pilot
as I am (or possibly particularly to such a poor pilot as I am)—the
weather matters. If I went to a weather predictor and he said, "I'm
a very sage man and I've been sitting here watching the clouds; yes,
it is safe for you to fly back to Chicago," I think I would decide that
it would probably be quicker for me to cut my throat. In fact, the
weatherman follows a rather different and much more complex
process. He has collected a massive amount of information over a
time about different configurations of weather, and he expresses his
propositions as percentages. I submit that the same should be true
of human behavior. They, too, should be advanced as similar statistical propositions. Every prediction that you make about human
behavior is in fact a prediction about the extent to which the person
being considered matches a group whose behavior you believe you
have observed in the past. You relate your knowledge of the individual to your acquired knowledge and experience about people most

nearly like him. A more accurate statement of the prediction is that, in your view, this man belongs to a group of which 60 will and 40 will not be involved in defined human behavior. You do not know, of course, whether he belongs to the 60 or to the 40. Despite these sometimes recognized imprecisions in their predictive capacities, psychiatrists remain deeply involved in predicting, for sexual psychopath laws, for sentencing, and for paroling. Increasingly, they are relied upon by judges who are happy to pass off at least a part of this difficult burden of foresight. Psychiatrists are being used as the doorkeepers; the doorkeepers to freedom. My brief plea, at this stage, is that you should consider the wisdom of pressing towards a greater refinement, by statistically valid methods, of your capacity to predict dangerous behavior, however it be defined. We must get rid of the usual dialogue between the judge and the psychiatrist which goes something like this: "Doctor, is he dangerous?" Reply: "He's psychotic." And sometimes the judge and the doctor think that they have talked to one another!

## PSYCHIATRIC TREATMENT OF MENTALLY ILL CRIMINALS

As a final topic, let me briefly mention the psychiatrist's involvement in the treatment of mentally ill offenders. The first point that I would make is that the convicted criminal should remain an ordinary citizen in the eyes of those responsible for the mental health services of the state. If he becomes mentally ill, it should be entirely proper for him to go to a mental hospital as civilly committed, or in appropriate cases, as a voluntary patient. We should more effectively provide for the transfer of psychotic prisoners to the mental health program of the state, and, when cured, if it be appropriate, for the transfer back to prison.

But putting that principle aside, I find to my regret a scant involvement of psychiatrists in the treatment of mentally ill offenders. The most serious effort in that regard in this country is the institution in Patuxent, Maryland. The institution which is the world's pathfinder in this field is of course Herstedvester in Denmark. If you are interested in the work at that institution, you can find it excellently described in Georg Stürup's *Treating the "Untreatable"* published by

Johns Hopkins Press. All that I am pleading for at this stage is that more psychiatrists should move seriously into the work of treating the dangerous, psychologically disturbed prisoners in institutions. They have to cease serving as diagnosticians of the system and become the treaters of the most difficult cases. Now, I know that this is not particularly attractive work, nor particularly well remunerated; but the profession of psychiatry must create career lines for those who will undertake this important task.

## Chapter 2

# PSYCHOTROPIC DRUGS AND COURT COMPETENCE

LEO E. HOLLISTER

This paper groups the most commonly encountered drugs according to their action on the individual and presents the author's opinion, supported by research evidence, as to their likely effect on courtroom performance. Doctor Hollister's style is very straight forward and unencumbered by vague conclusions and fear of taking a position. His general impression is that rather than being a hindrance to standing trial, medication can more likely "enhance rather than reduce the court competence of defendants with true emotional problems." It is hoped that his presentation may be helpful in alleviating some of the confusion and lack of consensus that currently exists in this crucial issue.

EDITORS

IDEALLY, all parties in criminal litigation should be free of drugs. The world not being ideal, such is seldom the case. The prosecuting attorney may take nicotine during recess by smoking a cigarette. The defense attorney may take caffeine in a cup of coffee. And both of these worthies, as well as the judge, may have been recently exposed to beverages containing ethyl alcohol. A woman juror may have taken a proprietary medication for relief of her headache that probably contains at least three different pain-killing or mood-altering drugs. A male juror may have taken a sleeping tablet the night before and still have the drug in his circulatory system. If the defendant has been incarcerated prior to his trial, he may be more free of drugs than any of the other participants, or at least his drug history may be better documented.

## DEFINITION OF THE PROBLEM

The point is that almost everybody takes drugs that affect mental function or behavior. These drugs are taken, as illustrated above, both for social and medical reasons. Many of these drugs are self-administered, in the sense that the patient has prescribed them for himself, purchased them without benefit of medical prescription, and takes them as he deems fit. Despite such widespread use of drugs that may affect mental processes or behavior, only rarely do they impair one's ability to function "normally." Indeed, it may be argued that one might function far less well without the stimulating cup of coffee, or without relief of a nagging pain, or if exposed to acute nicotine withdrawal. Effects of drugs may be good as well as bad.

Court competence implies two aspects of the mental processes and behavior of someone brought to trial. First, he must be able to understand and appreciate how the legal proceedings may affect his welfare. Second, he should be able, within the limits of his ability, to assist actively in his defense. Thus, the defendant should not be subjected to negative prejudice because of any drug which he has been given or has taken.

## TYPES OF DRUGS LIKELY TO BE OF CONCERN

Some of the more commonly used drugs which could affect the mental processes or behavior of someone coming to trial fall into six categories.

### Stimulants

Coffee, tea, and cola beverages are the usual sources of the mild stimulant, caffeine. The effects of this drug are scarcely discernible unless it is taken in marked excess. More likely, the habitue' deprived of his morning coffee will feel listless and lackadaisical instead of his normal self. Stronger stimulants, such as dextroamphetamine, methylphenidate, methamphetamine, and pipradrol, are not likely to be given to a defendant before trial. Such drugs, including some not clearly identifiable as stimulants, such as phenmetrazine, mephentermine, or diethylproprion, might be administered to control appetite. Stimulants could be self-administered illicitly, even in prisons. In any case, their effects are not likely to cause impairment except at very high doses, when the attendant nervousness, restlessness, and distraction may be harmful. The usual effects of ordinary doses might be to increase one's feeling of well-being (though seldom to an inappropriate degree), to enhance normal mental functions briefly, and to allay fatigue.[1] Considering the unlikelihood that drugs of this type would be given in a quantity sufficient to cause impairment, their mere use should not reduce one's competence to stand trial.

## Hypnotics

These drugs are at the opposite end of the spectrum; instead of stimulating the nervous system, they depress it. The degree of depression, based largely on the dose, distinguishes between use of these drugs for calming nervousness (sedation) or for producing sleep (hypnotic action). Various barbiturates are commonly used in this way, such as secobarbital or pentobarbital sodium, as well as some so-called non-barbiturate drugs, such as glutethimide, ethchlorvynol, methaprylon, and chloral hydrate.[2] Many of these drugs are long-acting, a desirable attribute when one wishes to remain asleep all night. The duration of action is not only dependent on the dose but on the level of drug attained in the individual subject due to factors concerned with his size and the rate at which he metabolizes or excretes the drug. As individuals vary widely in these respects, doses of such drugs also vary, perhaps several-fold among different individuals. Further, people taking these drugs do not remain the same; after repeated doses, they may handle the drug differently, both in terms of its behavioral effects and in their ability to get rid of it. A defendant given an initial dose of such a drug during a trial might have enough residual daytime effect from the drug to impair his competence to stand trial, although this eventuality is remote.

## Analgesic Drugs

Such drugs are used for relief of pain. Pains coming from the skin structures, muscles, bones, or joints are often readily alleviated by milder analgesics which act primarily in these structures, such as aspirin.[3] Pains coming from body organs are usually more severe and require stronger analgesics which act on the brain, such as morphine.[4] It should be apparent that, except in doses so high as to cause toxic symptoms, most of the milder analgesic drugs of the aspirin type (acetaminophen and acetophenetidin are others) will cause no impairment. Even some drugs related to morphine, such as propoxyphene or codeine, are so weak that they are more properly classified with the mild analgesics and, like the latter, are unlikely to cause impairment except in considerable overdose. Drugs of the morphine type, which also include meperidine and pentazocine, would only be likely to be used in such severe medical conditions as to preclude trial due to other medical considerations.

## Antianxiety Drugs

These are new chemicals but old drugs. The aim of sedation is to calm one down, to tranquilize, to relieve anxiety. This name has been applied to new chemicals which share many of the pharmacological properties of the hypnotics and sedatives.[5] Meprobamate, chlordiazepoxide, and diazepam are the principal antianxiety drugs. In addition, a number of antihistaminic drugs with sedative properties have also been revived for this use, such as diphenhydramine and hydroxyzine, as well as many that are sold without prescription. The same principles apply with this class of drugs as with the hypnotics and sedatives. As these drugs are usually given on a chronic basis, some degree of tolerance to their effects usually occurs after several days, so that chances of impairment should be minimized. Conversely, by allaying anxiety, they may make the defendant more fit to stand trial than he would have been in an untreated state.

## Antidepressants

These new drugs for treating depressed mental states are somewhat controversial, although in some cases of severe depression they undoubtedly afford much needed relief. A common misconception, based upon their ability to change a slowed down, dull person into one who is active and bright, is that they are stimulants. Most of the commonly used antidepressants, such as imipramine, amitriptyline, desipramine, and nortriptyline, are sedating rather than stimulating and, in single doses, often act like sleeping tablets. Besides possible impairment from their sedative effect, another undersirable pharmacological effect is that of blocking cholinergic nervous system transmission, that is, that mediated by acetylcholine. Such anticholinergic effects may cause mental confusion or delirium, especially in older persons who may be especially sensitive to these adverse mental effects. As these toxic symptoms occur subtly and are intermittent, they may be missed. [6] Their presence would decrease one's competence to stand trial, but so would severe mental depression of a degree which merited treatment. As it is usually a matter of three to four weeks before much amelioration of depression occurs with these drugs, during which time adverse mental symptoms are likely to become obvious, at least this amount of time should elapse before anyone requiring treatment with these drugs is brought to trial.

## Antipsychotics

These new drugs for treating patients with schizophrenic reactions are extremely powerful agents which should be reserved for treating patients with severe degrees of emotional disorder.[5, 6]   A defendant considered to be actively schizophrenic may not be competent to stand trial, but it is possible that treatment with these drugs for several weeks might control his psychosis to the extent that he may be declared competent. In such a case, he may seem much more rational in court than he was at the time of the criminal offense, possibly prejudicing his chances for a successful plea of insanity. Thus, to assure fairness to the defense, it should be emphasized that the defendant is not to be judged on his present status, which may have been considerably ameliorated by drugs, but on that described at the time of the criminal act. As these drugs are powerful sedatives, early in treatment some improvement in mental state may be negated by impairment from excessive sedation. These effects usually disappear after several weeks of treatment, either by the patient becoming accomodated to the drug or his physician's finding a suitable dosage schedule. At this time, beneficial effects from antipsychotic drugs might be expected to be clearly apparent. Although several chemical classes of antipsychotic drugs are used, phenothiazine derivatives are most widely employed. Some fifteen members of this drug class are on the market, those most widely used being chlorpromazine, thioridazine, and fluphenazine.

## GENERAL CONSIDERATIONS

As a rule, drugs of the types being discussed have their greatest impact on normal mental processes during the initial doses. That is, the first dose or two of any central nervous system depressant is likely to impair the patient far more than the twenty-fifth dose, even though these may be the same amount. This phenomenon is due to the ability of human beings to compensate for drug-induced impairment of a fairly high degree (although obviously far from perfect in many users of ethyl alcohol). It is also due to the fact that during continued use of a drug, the body develops more efficient machinery for disposing of the drug so that, with most dosage schedules, the drug exists in the body in a fairly narrow range of concentrations. Such "steady-state" conditions are determined by the time it takes the body to eliminate the drug and by the frequency of the dosage. However, for most of the drugs with which we are concerned, this condition is reached fairly soon. With the passage of time, the therapeutic effects of the drug may outweigh any disadvantages. Patients who are impaired in their functions after the initial doses of drug may be improved after a few weeks of treatment.

These considerations make it obvious that no court proceedings should involve a defendant who has recently been placed on a drug to which he is not habituated. Instead, time should be provided for accomodation to the drug. These time intervals may vary from a few days, in the case of antianxiety drugs or hypnotics, to a few weeks, in the case of antipsychotic drugs.

Another reason for delaying court proceedings is that persons charged with criminal acts may already be taking self-administered drugs in large amounts. Persons habituated to such large doses have already developed compensatory mechanisms and may appear to be normal. When they are deprived of drugs, they may experience withdrawal effects, the most dramatic being the delirium tremens experienced by subjects withdrawn from alcohol.[7] Withdrawal effects from opiate drugs, such as heroin, might be expected to occur within hours of the last dose; but in the case of some of the commonly used sedatives or hypnotics, they may not appear for two or three days. Thus, a person who appears to be normal when arrested might be quite abnormal when arraigned. As many of the drugs which produce such reactions can be detected by chemical examinations of blood or urine, it seems reasonable to make these examinations at the time of arrest to forestall marked withdrawal reactions.

As stated at the outset, ideally all parties to the legal process should be drug free. Whenever possible, medical use of drugs should be temporarily discontinued for individuals coming to trial. The situations will vary. Use of stimulant drugs to control appetite obviously may be stopped, while one would not dare to stop using antipsychotic drugs in a schizophrenic defendant.

Especially in those situations where drug therapy must be continued during trial, it would seem desirable to have a psychiatric determination of court competence made just prior to trial, when drugs are being administered in the customary doses. If the defendant is then regarded as competent, it is unlikely that such a determination would change during the trial, provided the dosage of drugs remains the same.

## CONCLUSIONS

Treating defendants in criminal actions with drugs is no different from treating anyone else; only the special circumstances are different. After many years of experience with these drugs, it seems clear that when properly used they are more likely to be beneficial than harmful, and more likely to enhance rather than reduce the court competence of defendants with true emotional problems. By applying some general rules in regard to the use of the various types of drugs, with an awareness of their special actions, one should be able to make a valid, common-sense judgment of court competence.

## REFERENCES

1. Martin, W. R., Sloan, J. W., Sapira, J. D., and Jasinski, D. R.: Physiologic, subjective and behavioral effects of Amphetamine, Methamphetamine, Ephedrine, Phenmetrazine, and Mathylphenidate in man. *Clin Pharmacol Ther*, 12:245, 1971.
2. Goodmen, L. S., and Gilman, A. (Eds.): *The Pharmacological Basis of Therapeutics*, 4th ed. New York, Macmillan, 1970.
3. Beaver, W. B.: The pharmacological basis for the choice of an analgesic. II. Mild analgesics. *Pharmacology for Physicians*, 4. Philadelphia, Saunders, 1970.
4. Beaver, W. B.: The pharmacological basis for the choice of an analgesic.

I. Potent analgesics. *Pharmacology for Physicians*, 4. Philadelphia, Saunders, 1970.

5. Hollister, L. E.: Clinical use of psychotherapeutic drugs: Current status. *Clin Pharmacol Ther, 10:*170, 1969.

6. Caffey, E. M., Jr., Hollister, L. E., Kaim, S. C., and Pokorny, A. D.: *Drug Treatment in Psychiatry*. Washington, D. C., Veterans Administration I B 11-2, 1970. (Available from Supt. of Documents, U.S. Government Printing Office, Washington, D.C. 20402. Price 40 cents).

7. World Health Organization: Expert Committee on Drug Dependence. *WHO Tech Rep Ser, 273,* 1964; *312,* 1965; *407,* 1969.

## Chapter 3

# THE PSYCHIATRIST AS A FRIEND OF THE COURT

### Jonas R. Rappeport

Doctor Rappeport describes the role of the psychiatrist as *amicus curiae*, a friend of the court. In such a role, the position of psychiatrist is not particularly that of a participant in the adversary system, but allows him to provide the best possible recommendations to the court. He is, therefore, removed from having to take sides, or at least from being represented to be on the side of the defense or the prosecution. In such instances, his concern is only that of presenting a valid psychiatric opinion, some reasonable medical alternatives, and their likely psychiatric consequences. In this paper, Doctor Rappeport describes in some detail the functioning, organization, and breadth of responsibility of the Medical Office of the Supreme Bench in Baltimore. The reader is thus presented with an in-depth description of the actual functioning of such a facility. This is followed by two case histories illustrating how "a friend of the court" can serve the patient and society.

EDITORS

THE subject of this paper will be the expert psychiatrist and his justification in considering himself *amicus curiae*, a friend of the court. You will read about the history, structure, and functioning of the medical office of the Supreme Bench of Baltimore. A few cases will be described, and then you will be told about some of the other areas in which we are involved.

*Webster's New Collegiate Dictionary* says that a friend is one who is attached to another by affection or esteem. Mark Twain once said, "There ain't no surer way to find out whether you like people or hate them, than to travel with them." In a sense, you might say that I have been travelling with judges for about twelve years. To borrow from another context, "Some of my best friends are judges." The concept of a friend of the court seems to be borrowed from the

Latin *amicus curiae*. This is usually seen where special parties are allowed to submit briefs to the appeals court to bring forth certain facts of law or interpretations of law that might not otherwise be heard.

As far as the trial court or the lower court is concerned, the precedent for judicial assistance is not entirely clear. Questions have been raised from time to time as to whether a lower court has the right to call upon its own experts. Wigmore says (speaking of the judge), "That he has no burden or duty of doing so is plain in the law. But the general judicial power itself expressly allotted in every state constitution, implies inherently a power to investigate as auxiliary to the power to decide: and the power to investigate implies necessarily power to summon and to question witnesses." In many of our personal experiences, there are situations where we wished that the judge might question us further and to a greater extent. There are apparently time-honored reasons why judges do not do this. However, it is clear that the judge is considered to have the right to call his own expert witnesses. This is particularly so when the judge is concerned because of varying testimony and when there is much disagreement. In legal situations relating to mental health issues, this situation arises as much, if not more, than in many other types of testimony. This disagreement has been going on for at least the past 150 years and, despite our strong feelings about it, will probably continue.

It is not new to anyone that it has been argued back and forth as to who is an expert and what makes the best expert. Although this is not the issue of my presentation, I would like to make my position clear. For a change, I had the very good fortune of being quoted correctly by the press. In an article in the *Baltimore News American* with reference to pretrial testimony, I said:

> Such medical-legal dilemmas have forced us to subvert ourselves into saying things in court which do nothing to help a person who needs medical treatment. We psychiatrists are in a difficult role. We have to say things like, "He didn't mean it," when in fact, we know that a person did, albeit his unconscious may have dictated the behavior. That is where medicine comes in. We have spent far too much good, learned, scholarly, well-intentioned time as experts for either side, the defendant or prosecution, or by the court even as its

own expert, to try and figure out whether a person is responsible at the
time of the crime, when our real job as physicians is to treat people.
Our job as forensic psychiatrists, in particular, should be to increase
our ability to predict dangerous behavior and to devise better methods
of treating offenders. I'm willing to agree at times it is necessary for
us to try and figure out if someone can stand trial or not. But even
the guidelines here, as was very clear today, are so ill defined that
perhaps it is a matter better decided by a jury anyway. I basically
feel that the best use of psychiatrist that society could make today is
*not* to have them testifying in a courtroom as to the mental responsibility
of a defendant at the time of his alleged crime.

Unfortunately, one may note that I did not say clearly what
the best use should be, only what it is not. In essence, I agree with
the statements that Dr. Karl Menninger has made in his book, *The
Crime of Punishment*, with reference to psychiatrists not testifying
in court. Nevertheless, I do so. I fortunately do not have to testify
too often, but I have been called on to do so. And I am not willing
to go on strike, because I am not ready to offer society a better
solution. Part of what may be a better solution is what I mostly do
in my work, what I like best to do, and that which Doctor Menninger
thinks we obviously should. This is the concept of using the expert
after the trial to assist the judge in disposition. I believe the basis
for this stands on firm ground.

In the early 1930's, the American Bar Association recommended
that there be available to every criminal and juvenile court, a
psychiatric service "to assist the court in the disposition of offenders."
As early as 1925, Sheldon Glueck and later Winfred Overholser
advocated that the courts rule only on the issue of whether or not
the offender had committed a crime and that a tribunal of psychiatrists, sociologists, and other experts be allowed to assist the judge in
proper disposition.

That is a good statement, but again my own personal opinion is
that we have a long way to go before we can say that we are prepared to fulfill that role. We have a long way to go in our expertise. I do not think we are in a position of saying, "We don't
know nothing," but I think we are in a position of saying we do
not know all that we should in order to accept such a serious responsibility as prescribing disposition.

In 1909, ten years after the first juvenile court was established in Chicago, Dr. William Healy became the first psychiatrist to work in any court clinic. Five years later, Dr. V. V. Anderson, helped to provide a psychiatric service for the Adult Court Clinic in Boston. These developments occurred 75 years after Isaac Ray's treatise. In the eyes of the law, which moves slowly, this was not a terribly long period of time; but in the eyes of psychiatry, which has moved rapidly, this was an awfully long period of time. In rapid succession, other court clinics were established in various jurisdictions, an adult clinic in Chicago in 1914, and a court clinic in Baltimore in 1918.

Each of the medical offices in the country, probably around 45 or 50, have started for different specific reasons. Consequently, each functions somewhat differently. Dr. Manfred S. Guttmacher said of these differences:

> Anyone surveying the organization or performance of court clinics must be struck by their diversity. There is no model and no set of standards. The *modus operandi* of each clinic must, at least in part, be affected by its origin. A clinic, brought into being as a result of community reaction to the sudden occurrences of a series of sexual crimes, is likely to continue to focus on such cases. Most of the court clinics are known as psychiatric or behavior clinics. The Baltimore clinic is designated as the Medical Office of the Supreme Bench and has certain non-psychiatric responsibilities.

For instance, we examine or arrange for the examination of nonsupport cases where the man claims he is physically disabled and cannot support his family; or, we will arrange for the examination of some of our older numbers writers who are sentenced to jail and say they cannot go to jail because they are physically ill. It seems that in Baltimore, the numbers operators hire older people, 70 or 75, to write numbers. When they are caught with a $1,000 book in their possession, they claim they have had a coronary or are severely hypertensive. How can you send them to jail for a year? This has really bothered some of our judges.

One of the most important developments during the past decade in court clinic organization was the establishment of a state-wide system in Massachusetts by the Division of Legal Medicine, Massachusetts Department of Mental Health. It was originally organized by Dr. Donald Hayes Russell and is currently under the direction of

Dr. Louis McGarry. There are now 17 clinics established in different circuits in Massachusetts with a tremendous full-time and part-time professional staff. There is also an aftercare clinic in Boston and psychiatric services are supplied to four correctional institutions. Almost all of these clinics provide treatment as well as diagnostic and advisory services. In 1956, the Toronto Court Clinics were established which at that time was unique in that it was associated with the outpatient division of a psychiatric hospital.

The history of the court clinic of Baltimore can best be told in the words of the first court psychiatrist, Dr. John Rathbone Oliver, who, in his autobiography called, *Four Square: the Story of a Four-Fold Life*, says:

> Like all really useful and permanent things, our service was a gradual development. It began at the very bottom of things in a small police court. At the time, in 1917, I was a member of the house staff of the Henry Phipps Psychiatric Clinic of the Johns Hopkins Hospital. Only a few squares from the hospital was our local police station and it happened that the magistrate who sat in that particular police court lived just across the way from Phipps Clinic. He was a rather unusual man and, on his way to or from the station house, he would often drop in at our dispensary to ask about an occasional police case that he had referred to us for diagnosis. He and I came to be rather good friend. He asked me to visit him at his court, and it soon became customary for me to sit close beside him when he was on the bench hearing cases. The next year I left the hospital and began private practice. Like all beginners, during the first year or two I had a good deal of free time, and I devoted most of it to my police-court work. But soon, thanks to one of the judges of our Supreme Bench who had been a classmate of mine at Harvard, I was brought into touch with the superior courts. Without his backing, our court medical service could never have been organized at all; for it was rough going in those days. However, every free moment, and I had many of them, I spent in the criminal courts. For two years I served the court without compensation as a sort of *amicus curiae*.

Thus, the Medical Office of the Supreme Bench had its beginning. To digress for a moment, Doctor Oliver was quite a special character. Besides being a psychiatrist, he was also an ordained Episcopal minister. Following his residency at Phipps, he obtained his Ph.D in Greek and became the Professor of the History of Medicine at the University of Maryland. He was a bachelor and he apparently was the warden of one of the dormatories at Johns Hopkins. He lived there for many years and probably started the first therapeutic community in America there, according to some of his stories. While working at the courts and in private practice, he became active in the church once again, and he used to hear confessions on Saturday night and sing the Mass every Sunday morning. I do not know whether there is a relationship between religion and the Baltimore Courts' psychiatrist, but Doctor Guttmacher, who succeeded Doctor Oliver, was the son of a rabbi. While I, who succeeded Doctor Guttmacher, have no such genuine religious credentials, am at least the Assistant Secretary and on the Board of Trustees of my congregation. I do not know whether or not it's a prerequisite for the job.

It would appear that our office was born from a heartfelt need by the judges for assistance in many different areas. The questions of ability to stand trial and responsibility at the time of the crime did not seem to occupy them since that is answered according to Maryland law, by the Department of Mental Hygiene. There is more opportunity for plea bargaining in Maryland since we have straight sentences rather than indeterminate sentences, as in many other states. This seems to lead the prosecutor and the courts towards a desire to make the penalty fit the criminal and not just the crime. This, it is thought, led in part to their concern for the best disposition for the defendant, whether he be a criminal or a domestic offender. Consequently, for these and other reasons, we have been very little involved in the pretrial issues. Perhaps, because of this, we can function in the friendly role that is not open to other court clinics or hospitals.

I will try to give you a clearer picture of how the Medical Office functions in this role. Our physical plant, that is our offices, are in the courthouse proper. While this may appear to be a minor point, it is very important in terms of communication with the court and all who are involved in the judicial process, as well as reflecting the esteem in which the court holds this office. I do think we get some reflection from the esteem of the court. We are also readily available to everybody. We are available for conferences with judges as well as defense attorneys and prosecutors and really anyone else who becomes involved in the case or happens to walk in the front door. We are also available for such emergencies as fainting or seizures. The story goes that Doctor Guttmacher once delivered a baby in the corridors of the courthouse.

We have a small but adequate staff to serve the City of Baltimore which has a population of slightly under one million. In our Adult Division we have a Chief and Assistant Chief Medical Officer, two Medical Officers under him, and two third-year resident psychiatrists from the University of Maryland (who spend one morning a week as an elective). We have a Chief Psychologist, Assistant Psychologist, and Consultants. Consultants represent professionals, for example a psychologist who has exceptional experience in the Rorschach, or another who is equally experienced in the Minnesota Multiphasic Personality Inventory. We also invite neurologists or other psychiatrists as consultants for specific cases where their expertise is needed. We have a psychiatric social worker who, to be honest, actually runs the office. She is the main person who schedules cases and maintains the major contact with the courts. Recently, we added two social work graduate students and we plan to expand our social work services. The social worker has the major contact with the courts because the Medical Officers, including myself, are only half-time while she is available on a full-time basis.

Like Doctor Oliver, Doctor Guttmacher had a private practice. He believed there could be a tendency in one who does full-time diagnostic work to become either a therapeutic hopeful or a therapeutic nihilist. He believed very strongly that one should be getting one's feet wet all the time. Therefore, the psychiatrists are all half-time and the psychologists are about three-quarter time. The staff is encouraged to become involved in community activities as well as private practice. We have only a small Juvenile Division since additional medical services are furnished the Juvenile Court by a separate state-operated Division of Juvenile Services. We have one Medical Officer in the Juvenile Court who is half-time, a psychologist who is a little more than half-time, and a secretary.

During fiscal year 1970, there were 816 referrals to the Medical Office. The Criminal Court sent 34 percent and the Municipal Court 31 percent. In Baltimore there is a Municipal Court which might be called the Magistrate Court, that is, the Police Station Court. It is a full-time, appointive and then elective judicial position. The judges, and attorneys, are paid very adequate salaries and serve for ten-year periods.

We also do emergency consultations at the Baltimore City Jail on any prisoner awaiting trial who appears to the jail physician to be psychiatrically ill. This source represented 18 percent of our cases in fiscal year 1970. Three percent of our cases come from other than the Criminal Division of the Circuit Court. These are generally custody cases from the Domestic Relations Court. The remaining 14 percent come from other sources, for example, the mailman whose wife is ill, or a police officer who has a problem with someone on his beat and comes in for consultation. Others come from the Pretrial Release Division. In Baltimore, we have a "release on your own recognizance" program. We must clear anyone who has a history of psychiatric hospitalization to reassure the court that this psychiatric history does not make the patient too dangerous to be released. The Probation Department also refers selected cases to us in order to assist their probation officer in handling their cases. Occasionally, the Traffic Court will ask for our assistance. The county courts, although they have their own psychiatrist, sometimes call on us.

In 1970, 12 percent of our work was pretrial or habeas corpus. Forty-seven percent, or the majority, of what we did was pre-sentence and not pretrial. In the examinations we make recommendations to the judge to assist him with disposition. Post-sentence examinations are those where a judge has already sentenced the person but has asked us to examine him. This type of examination represented 12 percent of our cases. In Maryland, the judge has a 90-day period to change his mind and may instead place the man on probation. He may think that he wants the man in prison to "sweat it out a little" while he asks us to see him or gathers other evidence which might indicate that a sentence is the best thing. Twenty-one percent were jail emergencies. Four percent were custody cases. One percent were competency exams in civil cases, that is, competency to handle one's affairs or what have you. In 3 percent of the cases, we only reviewed the records and offered an opinion on that basis.

The psychiatrist sees practically every case (Fiscal 1970, 789). The psychologist does not see every case (n=257). We have recently established a routine battery of take-it-yourself tests including an MMPI, sentence completion, and a House-Tree-Person test. Our secretaries score the MMPI and the psychologist gives a very brief report which is then discussed with the psychiatrist. This may be followed by more thorough testing if indicated. Our social worker, while involved in the entire process, does not see every case (n=207).

Table 3-I shows the types of offenses committed by those referred to us. Approximately 54 percent involved serious crimes of assault, murder, rape and attempted rape, robbery, and burglary and larceny.

TABLE 3-I

TYPES OF OFFENSES OF CASES REFERRED — 1970

| Offenses | Numbers | Percentages (%) |
|---|---|---|
| Assault | 317 | 27 |
| Murder | 46 | 4 |
| Rape & attempted rape | 44 | 4 |
| Robbery | 81 | 7 |
| Burglary | 90 | 8 |
| Larceny | 49 | 4 |
| Auto theft | 33 | 3 |
| Arson | 29 | 2 |
| Forgery | 13 | 1 |
| Fraud | 28 | 2 |
| Vandalism | 11 | 1 |
| Weapons | 39 | 3 |
| Prostitution | 1 | 0 |
| Sex offenses | 73 | 6 |
| Narcotics laws | 73 | 6 |
| Gambling | 1 | 0 |
| Offenses against family | 39 | 3 |
| Driving under influence | 2 | 0 |
| Liquor laws | 3 | 0 |
| Disorderly conduct | 63 | 5 |
| Vagrancy | 6 | 1 |
| Curfew | 2 | 0 |
| Runaway | 2 | 0 |
| Violation of probation | 16 | 1 |
| Prosecuting witness | 18 | 2 |
| All other offenses | 113 | 10 |
| Total* | 1192 | 100 |

* Includes multiple offenses.

Usually the burglaries and larcenies that we see have more serious aspects. The 5 percent in the disorderly conduct category were usually individuals whose disorderly conduct was actually a part of their mental illness. The reason we see many patients charged only with disorderly conduct is that such a charge is frequently used to allow the police to step in to assist the mentally ill, since we do not have a simple emergency commitment law in Maryland. While the Maryland law requires that a pretrial examination is to be conducted by the Department of Mental Hygiene, we frequently see such people when counsel approaches the judge and requests our office conduct the examination.

It has been mentioned that an indigent defendant does not have the right to have a court appointed psychiatrist. This places a hardship on the attorney who is not sure whether or not he should consider an insanity plea, yet does not want the Department of Mental Hygiene to make this judgment. He may come to see us. We may just talk with him and advise him what to do. If he wants us to see the defendant, we usually ask for an official order from the judge. We then may carry out a simple screening examination and advise him. We enjoy this role very much since we think that it reduces a waste of time at the hospital. We can screen those cases that have no merit for such examinations, or we can assist counsel by advising him as to a private psychiatrist he might want to employ. In fact, most of our leading criminal attorneys call on us when they have a case where an insanity plea may be indicated. They come to me early in their preparation of the case to discuss it with me so I can recommend what literature they might read in order to get a better understanding of the psychiatric approach, or I might recommend a psychiatrist they can employ to examine their defendant. They usually do this before filing an insanity plea.

We not only see cases for the judges and lawyers, but also the State's Attorney and others—even for the Welfare Department when the case will be of particular interest to us. Many cases come from the city jail where people are awaiting trial. Whenever a very, very bad crime is reported in the papers and the circumstances lead us to believe the perpetrator is mentally ill, we see him on our own as soon as possible. We see him and, if hospitalization is indicated, we speak to the State's Attorney and to his counsel and try to arrange to have the patient hospitalized. We are fortunate in the City of Baltimore that, regardless of the crime, if the person is obviously mentally ill, our prosecutors are very cooperative. On borderline cases, it may be different. The State's Attorney's job is to be the prosecutor. But, when it is quite clear that the person was ill, we have no difficulty with over-zealousness on the part of the prosecutor. Occasionally, in jail, we will pick up individuals whose attorneys have not recognized how ill their clients are and that their clients may not be reponsible. We then contact the attorneys immediately. On a few rare occasions, we have seen people for pre-sentence examinations where we thought that there was a good possibility that the person should never have been tried, because he may not have been competent to stand trial. Then, we generally call both the prosecutor and the defense in for a conference and discuss the situation with them. On occasion, they have had to go back to court and have the case stricken from the records. When our suspicions are not strong, counsel may decide not to raise the issue. We feel uneasy at times since we are not sure where our responsibility should stop.

The staff at the state hospitals frequently disagrees and we are then called on as the "super expert." They are required by law when they have a disagreement in their staff as to criminal responsibility or ability to stand trial to report this and, of course, the prosecution and the defense each pick the psychiatrist for his side. Then, the court will call on us to be super experts. I do not like the role of super expert. Both Goldstein, from Yale University, and Diamond, from San Francisco, have written excellent articles about experts and the extra weight given to staff conferences or the super expert. We think we do have to function in this role and when necessary we function that way. Because of our *amicus* position we rarely testify. With 800 cases we testified seven times in fiscal year 1970. Perhaps this means that the judge does give our opinions undue weight. This may be true. I hope that it is not because I am not sure that my opinion should be given such strong weight as compared to others.

Regardless of what question is asked, we obtain as much information as possible. This includes the police arrest record with any statements of the defendant and witnesses, court testimony if transcribed, and hospital and doctor's reports. Our social worker will interview the parents or spouse and sometimes the neighbors. We have even brought in police officers who have made the arrest. We do psychological tests when indicated and special examinations, such as electroencephalograms or neurologic examinations.

We send an open report to the court in all pretrial cases. The report includes only what is absolutely necessary. That is, if we think that the individual is responsible, we so indicate. If he is competent, we say so without further explanation. However, we then send the courts, under seal, a complete report with all the information along with recommendations for disposition. I think this is terribly important and want to talk about it further.

I am told that, on several occasions where recommendations for disposition have been included in a pretrial report, courts have criticized the hospitals and have said, "If I wanted your advice on this matter, I would have asked for it." This usually occurs when the hospital or doctor has included pre-sentence recommendations in the body of the pretrial report. If you consider yourself a forensic psychiatrist, then you should know better, because this is telling the judge something he may not know at that time. He may not know all of your hearsay ideas. He may not know that you think this individual should go to jail because he has been in jail three other times unless that is brought out during the trial. He may know it after the trial. While you should not include this in the body of a pretrial report, I think you should, even must, include it under seal in a separate report.

In traveling around the country and even in some of our own hospitals in Maryland, that is not the practice. Hospital administrators and psychiatrists seem to defer all too readily to the courts. One judge says, "Don't do that, how dare you!" It is never done again. We play the institutional game. If you ask about it a year later you will be told that not only has it never been done, but that one psychiatrist tried to do it and got six months for contempt of court. The myth has started. There is absolutely no reason that I know of why we should not do this. The issue is how much information should be furnished the court in a pretrial report. I think that we should say at the bottom of a pretrial report something to the effect, "As is our practice, after examining the defendant thoroughly we enclose, under seal, a complete report which the court may use for the purposes of disposition should he be found guilty of the crime or not guilty by reason of insanity." Of course, you have to remember the patient should know that the information you are getting from him may be used in sentencing, not just in the pretrial determination. After all, we spend hours evaluating him, observing him, and having staff conferences in a hospital—30, 60, 90 days. Are we going to devote all this time and then only write a brief report saying the defendant is responsible and competent to stand trial? Is disposition not the area in which we wish to work? Are the questions of disposition not the questions we are most competent to answer?

If we would like the court to recognize that we have good advice, we have to offer it to them. If we believe that we have good ideas with reference to the future care and treatment of the offender and the protection of society, then let us stand up and speak accordingly. I think we have to let the judge shout if he does not like it. I doubt if any judge would ever issue an order forbidding a hospital from sending him a report under seal. If he does not want it, then let him dispose of it. I think that it is criminal for any Department of Mental Hygiene, in this time of short money and limited professional staff, to allow its staff not to give the court all the advice and information that is available. There are, however, two very important considerations. First, we cannot become angry or discouraged if the court does not follow our recommendations. Second, our advice must be realistic. As far as advice goes, Ralph Waldo Emerson said, "I do then with my friends as I do with my books. I would have them where I can find them, but I seldom use them." The judge has heard testimony, he has seen the defendant in the courtroom, he has seen the witnesses, he has seen the victim, and he has heard policemen testify. He has heard a lot of things that we have not heard. He can reflect the community's reactions and feeling much better than any psychiatrist. This is an important part of his role. Therefore, we should not become angry if he does not accept our very good, well-reasoned, timely advice.

In order for our advice to be realistic, our reports have to make good sense. Our recommendations must be well thought out and reasonable. At times, we can be innovative, but we must be practical. It is certainly foolish to recommend psychoanalysis for a farm boy who had an I.Q. of 85. You know he cannot use it. He cannot afford it and he cannot get it. It's just as foolish to recommend intensive long-term, outpatient psychiatric treatment at the local county mental health center when everybody knows that the clinic has a waiting list two years long and that they are not providing any intensive long-term psychotherapy. This, then, places a tremendous responsibility on us to know what facilities exist within the correctional system and within the community to which the person might return. We must not make wild recommendations.

On the other hand, we also have the opportunity to do a little proselytizing. You know, judges are very influential people. Every once in awhile in our reports we might say something like this:

> This man would be an excellent candidate for an outpatient treatment facility offering group therapy for special sex offenders. We think a group therapy outpatient program similar to the ones that exist in Philadelphia, Oklahoma City, and Toronto would be just the thing this man needs. These facilities report excellent results in similar cases. Without such treatment, this man will probably repeat his offenses again and again. Unfortunately, no such facility exists in our community. Therefore, we recommend that he be sentenced to prison.

After the judge reads a few of these he may become your advocate. When you meet him at a conference somewhere and he says, "Hey Doc, when are we going to get one of those facilities?" Then I say, "When you tell the newspapers we need one." If there is a reporter in court, sometimes the judge will read such comments from your report if he is frustrated about it. Slowly, things come about. I know from reading many of Doctor Guttmacher's old reports that statements such as this were one of the things that were responsible for the creation of the Patuxent Institution in Maryland. Once the ball got rolling, it just rolled along.

I want to give you a brief summary of two cases in order to let you see how I think they might stir up some controversy as to whether our recommendations were correct or not. I'm not offering them as the best clinical judgments.

## Case I

This case involves a 51-year-old man charged with perverted practices (Sodomy) on a 10-year-old boy. His attorney interviewed him, went to the judge, and said "Your Honor, my client tells me that he had an operation on his penis for priapism and since then he has not been able to get an erection. He says he has no nature and, therefore, he could not possibly have committed the offense." Next, we received a referral stating these facts. Ordinarily, for a medical problem we would have sent him to the urology clinic, received a report back, and interpreted it to the court. But we thought that this was a rather unique case and we also knew, of course, the fact that he could not get an erection had nothing to do with whether he might have or might not have tried to commit sodomy. In fact, it might make him want to try all the more. On the other hand, we recognized that for legal reasons this might be very important. So we did what we ordinarily do—we found out what hospital he had been in for his operation and sent for the hospital records. We also asked for the local police department's arrest record as well as the state's attorney file in the case which included the police officer's report of the incident. The hospital report said, "Priapism, cause undetermined, spontaneous recovery, no surgery." So we, therefore, knew that he had not had an operation and was not necessarily impotent. The arrest record revealed a 1961 arrest for disorderly conduct resulting in hospitalization in a state hospital and the same in 1969.

We then arranged to see him in our offices. He had been released on his own recognizance and was back working in the manufacturing plant where he had been employed on and off for the past 30 years. He had a very responsible position there pouring hot steel. As soon as he came into my office, he began to tell me a story that proved to be very interesting. It seems that in 1953, he separated from his wife. At that time, he was called to the Welfare Department by a State's Attorney (Mr. A.) who was assigned to the Welfare Department. Mr. A. told him that he had to pay some money or else he would go to jail. Mr. A. also suggested that our patient raped a white woman, but he said he talked Mr. A. out of that. Mr. A. then wanted him to join a gang of Mr. A's to steal things from stores. But then he talked him out of that. Then Mr. A. threatened him and told him he was going to get him charged with petty larceny. But the patient said that that's child's stuff and I just told him he wouldn't consider doing that. Since then Mr. A. has been tormenting him and affecting him in all sorts of ways. He has a machine which allows the patient to hear Mr. A. talking from the house next door and allows Mr. A. to know what he is thinking all the time.

I will not go into any great detail. We asked him about the victim in the case. He said that the boy really had nothing to do with it. There was nothing. He knows the boy. The boy lives in the neighborhood. He sees the boy all the time but that he feels certain that somebody had given a man money to get the boy to make this charge against him.

I then called the attorney and asked him if he had ever talked to his client. He assured me that he had talked to him at length. Apparently, either not long enough or else the patient thought that such "medical information" was not for the ears of his attorney, since the lawyer denied knowing any of this. I believed him since I was certain that had he known he would have filed an insanity plea.

We did a complete workup and found the following: He had been married briefly in 1953, but had left his wife after several months because he was sure that she had at one time committed murder and had served time in prison and he was afraid of her. Within a year or two after that, he was quite psychotic and was hospitalized in a state hospital where he remained for the better part of three and a half years with very brief visits home. In 1960, he was placed on convalescent leave and seen by the out patient clinic. In 1961, and 1969, he was readmitted for short periods, via the police, on a disturbing the peace charge. Otherwise, he has been outside working regularly, taking 500 mg of phenothiazine a day. He maintains contact with his siblings and lives alone in a room. He eats out because he is afraid that if he eats at home somebody will poison his food—Mr. A. that is. If he eats in a restaurant he thinks the food is safe.

Here is a citizen who, while working regularly and supporting himself, is probably known as the neighborhood oddball. Other than this offense, to our knowledge, he has never done any other harm. Was he responsible at the time of the crime? Maryland uses the Model Penal Code test. Is he competent to stand trial? Is he dangerous to himself or others? We discussed the case and came to some tentative conclusions but we believed we wanted to get a little more information so we asked the prosecutor to interview the victim and see if he could shed some light on the actual offense. Following this, we had a conference with his lawyer and the prosecutor. We asked his counsel if, in view of all of this, did he think that his client was able to stand trial? In essence, we felt that he was not responsible at the time of the crime and that he was competent to stand trial. In Maryland, we are very fortunate in that our law is such that the court may, after finding him not guilty by reason of insanity, send the man to the state hospital for evaluation as to his dangerousness. After 90 days, if the hospital reports that he is not too dangerous to release, they may, with the court's approval, release the man to an outpatient status and maintain supervision over him for at least five years. We were comfortable going this route. We did not want to take this man out of the community permanently. We did not think he was really that dangerous. On the other hand, and his counsel agreed, we wanted to have some control over him because we were not quite sure what had been going on recently to cause him to commit his offense if he, in fact, did commit it. We thought we wanted some supervision and it would best be accomplished by the maximum security hospital outpatient clinic which had a greater sensitivity and sense of responsibility for such patients.

We must recognize that there are psychiatrists and psychiatrists; clinics and clinics. When dealing with people who have committed offenses, we need a certain type and quality of supervision. A different approach may be required as opposed to the neurotic patient who does not have any serious acting-out behavior and who willingly comes to the clinic. Every outpatient clinic and every psychiatrist is not equipped to deal with this type of problem. We must recognize this and I believe we have a responsibility as forensic psychiatrists when making a recommendation for outpatient treatment that the facility we recommend is one which will recognize the problem and be able to deal with it in an adequate manner.

## Case II

I will only discuss the second case briefly. Initially, we saw this 18-year-old boy after he was found on the rooftops confused and incoherent. This experience was related to the sniffing of dry-cleaning fluid. At that time, our report indicated that he was an impulsive adolescent struggling with problems of growing up and making an adequate male identification. There was no evidence that he had been an extremely aggressive individual although he had been in some previous minor difficulties. There was a history of his being treated by a neurologist because of fainting spells which were described as epileptic seizures of an unusual type. His electroencephalogram revealed a 14/6 pattern, a pattern that is not clearly understood but frequently seen in acting-out delinquents and may be a normal artifact of adolescence. Nevertheless, he certainly was emotionally unstable. We said, "He may well get into further trouble, but we suggest that he be placed on probation with the condition that he attend an outpatient clinic at the Psychiatric Institute and take medicine prescribed and that his mother, who is quite involved in much of his difficulty, be encouraged to continue in the group therapy program in which she has been involved." However, we later discovered that after we saw him he was charged with a perverted practice on a 14-year-old girl whom he supposedly grabbed and knocked down and on whom he unsuccessfully attempted to perform cunnilingus. This offense supposedly occurred prior to our seeing him although there had been no mention of it by him. As a result thereof, we were asked to see him again. At that time, we reviewed our material and the records of the clinic. He had been attending clinic fairly regularly and taking his medication and had been working for a sign company for the four months before we saw him the second time. His mother, however, had been quite ill and had not been able to follow through with group therapy. He denied the offense and stated that he was convicted on a description of him by the victim. Since he denied the offense, he could not tell me anything about it. In reporting back to the court, I stated that despite the new offense my impressions remained the same. I thought he was an impulsive individual and that he would probably get into further difficulty, that some of the impulsiveness may be accounted for on a neurological basis and certainly some on a psychological basis, and I thought that he was showing some response to the treatment previously recommended and suggested that his outpatient probation program be continued. While his impulsivity concerned me, I continued to think that he was not seriously dangerous. The court requested that members of my staff testify at the disposition hearing and with great reluctance accepted our recommendations but insisted that we personally keep an eye on the situation. That is, to follow through with his treatment and keep in contact with the clinic to be sure he was following his treatment commitment. While the Probation Department usually does this, the court thought that the seriousness of this case along with its peculiar medical features warranted our supervision.

We have heard two examples of how a friend of the court can function readily and easily with the court in very borderline and questionable cases. I particularly chose these two cases because I am quite sure that many will think that our judgment was much too liberal and lenient and that these individuals might well have been incarcerated. In a certain sense, we see our job as an attempt to find other alternatives to incarceration without placing the community at too great a risk.

We also are involved in other areas. We are intimately involved with the Johns Hopkins Medical School and with the University of Maryland's Law School, School of Social Work, and Medical School. We give consultations, lectures, and case presentations. We consult with the Department of Corrections and Department of Parole and Probation. Interestingly enough, the court wishes us to perform these functions. When I came to the court they told me that this was part of my role. Our entire staff is very active in legislative matters, not necessarily as members of the court family but as individuals, and we think we try to function in a role of friendship to all.

I have talked a great deal about law and courts. I would like to say in closing that I think to be a judge is probably one of the loneliest roles in the world and that he needs all of the freinds that he can find.

## Chapter 4

# THE CHICAGO ELEVEN TRIAL AND ITS PSYCHIATRIC IMPLICATIONS

### WERNER TUTEUR

As a forensic psychiatrist with many years of experience, Doctor Tuteur is able to capably address himself to the issues and problems confronting the psychiatrist called upon to participate in trial proceedings. He selected the widely publicized Chicago Eleven Trial as an example of the sometimes difficult and complicated issues confronting an expert witness. In that trial, several of the defendants used a defense of "cultural insanity." Doctor Tuteur concluded that the lack of success with such a defense "proved that psychiatry has not reached the state where it can be used and abused at will for the purpose of a defense in a criminal proceeding."

EDITORS

THE Chicago Seven Trial was conducted with much fanfare and dealt with the Chicago riots during the 1968 Democratic Convention. In its wake followed the Chicago Eleven Trial dealing with defendants who had burned draft records on May 25, 1969. The incident occurred outside a Chicago South Side Selective Service Office. It was staged during the evening hours and the defendants waited for the authorities to arrive. The defendants were subsequently arrested. The trial was conducted in the Federal Court of the Northern District of Illinois, Eastern Division, Chief Judge Edwin A. Robson, presiding.

The charges against the defendants were destruction of government property, mutilation of government records, interfering with the Selective Service System, and conspiracy.

The trial began in early May of 1970, and it lasted through the first week of June. Psychiatry played an important part inasmuch as four of the eleven defendants labored under their self-made thesis that "if the Indochina War is insane, then burning draft records must be sane in order to avoid further bloodshed and an atomic holocaust in this country. If 'normal' people think that the opposite is true, then *we* must be 'insane'." This philosophy led to their concept of "cultural insanity." The defendants tried to indicate that what is right within one culture (their own), may be wrong within another, and vice versa. The federal courts accept the concept of insanity as a defense based only on clinical findings and accepted psychiatric diagnosis. The author entered the trial, court appointed, on motion of the prosecution.

The prime mission of the examinations was to determine the defendants' competency to stand trial. The examinations were conducted on May 29 and 30, 1970, at the Offices of the United States Attorney in Chicago.

Three defendants were male and one was female. They belonged to a militant movement which condemns drug abuse. All four were Catholic; one was a priest. They ranged in age from 19 to 40. All of them had attended college and two held degrees.

All of them excelled in politeness and were fully cooperative during the examinations. All were and remained in full contact with reality and were individuals given to high ideals and strong convictions, who talked very convincingly. Naturally, they abhorred the present Vietnamese conflict, were willing to fight for their convictions, would accept hardship to implement them, and were even willing to face deprivation of their personal freedom, if needed. They were in opposition to the present U. S. Government and its representatives.

The four were fully able to understand the nature and purpose of the proceedings against them and were able to assist in their defense. This, in the absence of a "mental condition," rendered them legally competent to stand trial. A diagnosis, "318 No Mental Disorder," was made for all four of them. The issue of their mental state with regard to criminal responsibility at the time of committing the act was later dealt with hypothetically, in open court, by direct and cross-examination. Using the four longitudinal histories, which were free of any kind of psychiatric disease, and based on the defendants' present mental state, the (hypothetical) defendants were considered to be criminally responsible for their conduct. They had

had substantial capacity either to appreciate the criminality of the conduct or to conform their conduct to the requirements of law. A jury so decided and found them guilty.

Clinical psychiatry *was* to enter the trial, however. One of the defendants, excluding the four who had claimed cultural insanity as a defense, had shown absurd behavior in open court and his counsel was having difficulties with him to such a degree that he claimed the defendant was unable to assist in his defense. He was also examined by the author. He was a 32-year-old, single male with a history of previous "nervous breakdowns." For years, he had been unable to follow a logical stream of thought and his verbalizations were fragmented. In short, signs of a probably long standing schizophrenic illness indicated that he was unable to assist effectively in his defense.

The trial was then interrupted and a competency hearing was held, resulting in the court finding this (fifth) defendant legally incompetent and remanding him to the Medical Center for Federal Prisoners, Springfield, Missouri, simultaneously declaring a mistrial for this defendant. He is to be tried after reaching legal competency.

As a whole, the Chicago Eleven Trial showed a flurry of ironic developments. The one defendant found to be incompetent to stand trial on grounds of mental illness was *not* one of the four who had claimed "cultural insanity." *His* psychiatric examination was requested by the defense, who was aiming at an acquittal of this particular defendant by reasons of insanity ("conventional" not "cultural" insanity, that is). The defense later opposed the commitment order to the Medical Center for Federal Prisoners. Furthermore, it developed that clinically the ideations of the four who did claim "cultural insanity" were well-founded in reality with regard to their strong convictions against the Vietnamese conflict and racism, leading to the clinical conclusion that their thinking *was* logical and their manner of speech extremely convincing, resulting in diagnoses of "No Mental Disorder." Their ways and means of implementing their ideas were antisocial, but *not* psychotic. Finally, two of the self-proclaimed "culturally insane" defendants failed to appear prior to the testimony of the psychiatrist and are presently being sought on fugitive warrants. Another defendant failed to appear the day following psychiatric testimony, although he did not participate in the "cultural insanity" claim.

Originally, 15 persons were arrested around a bonfire of draft records. Four of the 15 never appeared for trial, leaving a balance of 11 as legal proceedings began. One defendant was found incompetent during the trial, two escaped before the psychiatrist took the stand, and another one absented himself, diminishing the total to seven by the time the jury started deliberation. All seven were found guilty and were sentenced to five to ten years.

The trial proved that psychiatry has not reached the state where it can be used and abused at will for the purpose of a defense in a criminal proceeding. The four defendants claiming "cultural insanity" were clinically highly motivated and adhered to strong convictions of their own. They were diagnosed as "No Mental Disorder." The manner with which they tried to implement their ideals was found to be illegal by the jurors. Others called the issue of "cultural psychiatry" a "gimmicky idea" and a "stunt," which in reality is preventing true dialogue pertaining to the issue .

Finally, the one defendant found incompetent to stand trial was suffering from a "legitimate" schizophrenic illness. The court acknowledged this and declared a mistrial, thus indicating that a truly progressive society excels in not prosecuting or sentencing the mentally ill.

## Chapter 5

# THE RIGHT TO TREATMENT AND THE INSTITUTION

Marvin Chapman

The central issue in Doctor Chapman's paper is whether individuals confined to a mental hospital have an enforceable right to treatment. A number of historical, philosophical, and legal antecendents are discussed in order to provide a broad perspective in which to interpret the emerging issues of "right to treatment." A number of crucial legal decisions have been handed down in the past few years. These are summarized and discussed in terms of the impact they had in moving our legal system to a strongly affirmative answer on the issue of whether patients have a right to such treatment. Doctor Chapman concludes that "the real significance of the 'right to treatment' concept is that it signals, for those with the wisdom to read it, that the basic rights of citizens will be extended into our institutions, and that institutional interference in any area of personal liberty will require justification."

EDITORS

IN recent years, those who are interested in the various interfaces between psychiatry and the law have found their interest drawn to the area involving the relationship between the public mental hospital and the involuntarily committed patient. This interface is currently dominated by the emergence of a newly articulated legal concept—the concept of the "right to treatment." The articulation of this concept has been carried out primarily by the courts, but, in fact, has implications which reflect a broader movement within our society. Thus, while this area has been primarily of interest to the forensic psychiatrist who is involved in hospital administration, and to the patient and his attorney, it is evident that a far broader spectrum of our society will be involved before the issues are resolved. The ripples of the Miranda Decision have spread far beyond the station-house interrogation room. So is it likely to be with the "right to treatment" issue.

The questions involved in this issue can be quite simply stated. The principal question presented by the courts to date has been, "If an individual is confined to a mental hospital, does he have an enforceable right to treatment?" Underlying this question is the contention that deprivation of liberty by confinement in a mental hospital carries with it society's promise of treatment for the mental disorder, the existence of which was used by society to justify the confinement. If we deprive a man of his liberty because he is "mentally ill," and, therefore, "dangerous to himself or others," are we promising to make a realistic and bona fide effort to treat him for that "mental illness?" What makes a mental hospital different from a jail? Does the fact that some places of confinement are specially labeled as hospitals require that the claims inherent in such a labeling actually must be honored? Are the laws that allow the operation of our mental hospitals, the commitment laws, based upon a legislative promise of treatment? Do the "indefinite commitment" features of "Sexual Psychopath" laws also rest upon such legislative expectation and promise? The "right to treatment" concept supplies an affirmative answer to these questions.

While this presentation will be oriented primarily toward the "right to treatment" issue concerning the committed mental patient, it must be recognized at the outset that this question is but a part of a larger question being considered in our courts and by those concerned with civil liberty in our society. This question is, "What is society's obligation to all individuals who are confined in institutions or whose liberties are restricted by society?"

It is apparent that while these questions are quite simple to ask, they involve extremely basic issues and the very complicated partnerships and patterns of responsibility, such that the answers that we seek are bound to be far from simple.

The problems involved in solving these riddles begin with the very basic matter of definition. We are currently witnessing within our society a broadbased and intensive struggle between those who hold differing opinions as to how society should handle a relatively well-defined group, the criminal, who is confined after performing specific illegal acts. The "right to treatment" issue concerning committed mental patients involves many of the same areas as the correctional issue, but is further complicated by the existence of even fewer common definitions of the affected group. Society stands in relative agreement on what constitutes an illegal act, but stands far from agreement on when a person is "mentally ill" or when a person is "dangerous." To make matters worse, the courts and the correctional system have been working in relative concert for many years and have established mechanisms for establishing definitions. The disciplines of law and psychiatry, on the other hand, are still discussing *if* they have something to contribute to each other and have not yet established where and when and how the partnership shall effectively operate.

We can begin our considerations by noting that society has traditionally reserved for itself the dominant position in any conflict with the individual. Individual rights generally have existed only as granted by society and only for the ultimate good of society. If society had what it believed to be justification, it imposed its will, hesitating only when society itself suffered or when there was controversy over what constituted adequate justification or over what constituted the "maximum good of society."

It was accepted very early that society had a right to protect itself and police its ranks, excluding from society, either by expulsion or incarceration, those who represented threats to society and punishing those who carried out antisocietal (antisocial) acts. Exclusion of individuals from society by confinement in institutions became associated at a very early phase with punishment for wrongdoing; and institutions, in general, became places where punishment was king and where humane treatment was not only unnecessary, but was actively to be avoided. The linkage between punishment and institution operation was established long ago.

It is not too surprising, then, that distinctions were lost and that it made little difference that the "protection of society" which justified the incarceration of a given individual was not for wrongdoing, but to prevent the spread of disease or to prevent dangerous acts springing from a diseased mind. To be sure, the ideas of the ancients about the causes of physical and mental disease fitted in rather well with these practices—mental illness was "possession by the devil" and could be cured only by imaginatively driving the devil from the hapless victim. It was unfortunate that physical suffering, disablement, and death (for the lucky ones, considering some of the imaginative "treatment" methods used) accompanied such efforts, but society had an obligation to do what it had to, what was necessary. The dehumanization, the profound neglect, and the degradation were not only considered appropriate for punishment or wrongdoing, they were also part and parcel of what was at that time accepted medical treatment. The operation of institutions was dominated by these practices and society became desensitized to and accepting of incredible and neglectful conditions within mental hospitals.

Judges, theologians, physicians, and philosophers were of one mind —society was fully justified in its manner of operation of its houses of detention. The responsible elements of society decreed and agreed that degradation was to be the natural state of affairs within institutions.

Such a union was durable and was disrupted only very gradually, as each discipline began to develop its own separate body of knowledge. The physician delineated himself from the priest, and became more scientist than "medicine man." This was a slow process and there is a significant question whether or not psychiatry in many areas has made the separation even to this day. Lawyers and judges separated their discipline from theology and participated in separation of governmental and religious power. Each discipline began to come of age and to reexamine some of the older "justifications" from the standpoint of new knowledge. Conflicts began to emerge and the task of maintaining a workable society became more complicated.

For an extended period of time, however, the operation of society's houses of detention was exempted from this process, as society felt no need to concern itself with what went on behind institution walls. Society remained unwilling to apply new knowledge to the plight of the inmate, preferring to rest with the old attitudes and the old practices.

However, even stone walls cannot halt progress forever and the attitudes of society began gradually to change. Punishment as a justification of confinement for the offender began to be eclipsed by the more enlightened concepts of rehabilitation. Courts began to take an interest in what happened after sentences had been pronounced. Statutes, and the courts administering those statutes, began to make clearer distinctions between the classes of individuals which society had traditionally confined and society began to reexamine this host of long-neglected areas.

Gradually, there was a growing recognition of the lack of differentiation which had become part of our institutional process. Those who were among the responsible governing elements in society began to realize what was occurring and that there was a very important difference between someone who was incarcerated because he had committed a crime and someone who was incarcerated because he was "mentally ill."

The earliest progress was made in the handling of the criminal offender. Each of these inmates had his day in court and occupied the center of the stage of the legal system. Inequities and inconsistencies became readily apparent and steps were taken to define and refine procedural and judicial safeguards. Progress, while slow, soon outstripped that made by less well-defined incarcerated groups. The juvenile, alcoholic, sexual psychopath, and "dangerous" mental patient were only tangentially the object of the courts' attention. The courts, understandably, displayed a reluctance to concern themselves with or invade the province of other disciplines.

When a man was committed to a mental hospital, the procedural route for his court hearing was not well defined and the bulk of these hearings traditionally were handled very informally. If a criminal offender wanted to disagree with the findings of the court, there was a readily defined process by which he could appeal his case. In commitment proceedings for mental illness, the court hearing was too often a dead end, with no prescribed route to the higher courts. The committed mentally ill patient was instead placed within the mental hospital system; thereby, being effectively placed beyond the effective protection and reach of the law. Patients were isolated socially, ineffective, and overwhelmed. The courts were quite ready to look into what the courts were doing, and even into what prison administrators were doing, but were not at all eager to go poaching into medical preserves.

This reluctance was so repeatedly demonstrated that mental hospital administrators, lawyers, and patients in mental hospitals have traditionally assumed and passively accepted that institution walls enclosed a special world wherein courts, policemen, and such did not exist. Documentation of this aspect is found repeatedly in psychiatric historical notes, in traditional practices of mental hospitals, and in many of the current cries of outrage uttered by hospital administrators who now face court inquiry and "intrusion."

In 1919, a state court was confronted by a group of men who, having contacted venereal disease, were involuntarily confined persuant to an act of the legislature which was designed to protect society by providing treatment for such individuals. Although the court acknowledged that the men had been ordered to the state penitentiary, it upheld their confinement, reasoning that since a wing of the prison had been renamed "State Quarantine Camp for Men," that their confinement was "not subject to the peculiar obloquy which attends" confinement in a penitentiary. Legislators and administrators took a wing of the penitentiary, changed the name on the door, and by that magic transformed it from a penal institution into a treatment institution. The court accepted this and would not pass that particular door. Similar reluctance was displayed in cases involving sexual psychopaths, narcotic addicts, and "defective delinquents," all members of groups which were subject to compulsory institutionalization under the rubric of rehabilitation and treatment, but which were denied the rights automatically granted to criminal offenders.

Gradually, however, the courts became less reluctant, and brought forth in 1956, the ruling in *Benton v. Reid*.[1]  In this case, the petitioner was suffering from chronic tuberculosis and was ordered indefinitely confined under the District of Columbia Quarantine Law, representing, therefore, another category of individuals deprived of liberty for the protection of society. Although he was being confined in the so-called "hospital wing" of the jail, the wing was no different from any other part of the jail (in a quite direct analogy to the previous case). Between 1919 and 1956, however there was a difference. The Court of Appeals held that Congress must have intended that persons so confined be sent to treatment facilities and not to penal institutions. Since the "hospital wing" of the jail did not meet this imputed promise, Benton had a right to be transferred to another facility or to be released.

In 1960, Dr. Morton Birnbaum, holding degrees in law and medicine, defined the concept of the right to treatment for the first time in an article published in the *Journal of the American Bar Association.*[2] He had been concerned with the indefinite incarceration of individuals within mental hospitals whose commitments were justified by the need to protect society from the dangerously mentally ill, but whose handling within the institutions was entirely devoid of any of the hallmarks of treatment. Doctor Birnbaum became an advocate of the rights of the committed patient and soon began to be sought out by patients seeking help. He described two of these cases at the Mental Hospital Institute held in Washington, D.C., in October 1968.

The first case involved a 60-year-old inmate of a Florida State Hospital who, subsequently, had 12 separate petitions for a hearing on the issue of the adequacy of his treatment denied by courts. What made this case particularly remarkable was that during the process of appeals, a legislative committee investigated the hospital where the petitioner was confined and found that there was only one doctor for the 1,000 inmates in that section of the institution, that the buildings were in a state of complete obsolescence (some being built before 1834), that disturbed inmates were commonly "choked down" to subdue them, and that some of the attendants, who gave care and treatment to the inmates, could neither read nor write. Doctor Birnbaum found, to his chagrin, that an inmate of a Florida public mental institution, his family, or his friends had no legal way to assure that he would receive proper care and treatment.

The second case involved a man who was 68 years of age and had been an inmate for more than 35 years at Creedmoor State Hospital, New York City. This inmate, too, had 12 separate attempts to have his case heard on the issue of inadequate care and treatment rebuffed by the courts, including three refusals by the United States Supreme Court. This was despite the fact that this inmate was one of more than 500 inmates in a section staffed by only one physician, producing a physician/patient ratio which was less than that in the surrounding area for the general public and less than that of Sing Sing Prison. In the entire year prior to his contact with Doctor Birnbaum, there was not even one note on his hospital chart by any physician, nurse, or attendant.

Hospital authorities denied that treatment was inadequate and petitions for a hearing were denied. During this same period, an elderly, bedridden inmate was found dead one morning—a victim of strangulation. This helpless man had been killed during a sexual assault by the attendant in charge of the ward at night whom, it turned out, had, for a long period of time, made a practice of routinely sexually assaulting helpless bedridden patients.

The importance of describing cases such as these lies, unfortunately, in describing conditions behind too many institution walls. These situations occurred in a modern era but are not unique, for these elements of neglect, degradation, and lack of respect for the patient as a human being, as well as respect for the patient as a citizen entitled to legal protection continue to extend into the present times. Thus, we can be sure that inquiry into the histories of most of our long-term institutions would unearth instances that were equally spectacular, where not only was the patient abandoned by the law, he was also abandoned by every other responsible segment of our society. The partnership between the legislature and judiciary in the formulation and application of the law, of the legislature and the psychiatrist-administrator in the funding and operation of the mental hospital, and of the psychiatrist and judiciary in the provision of medical-legal justifications for confinement were frequently combining not to help the patient, but to perpetuate the ancient attitudes and practices.

The mechanisms whereby each member of these interlocking partnerships was supposed to have an obligation to the patient failed. The legislator responded only to the needs of his noninstitutionalized constituents. He forgot completely about those who were "out of sight and out of mind." The courts viewed their work as done when the public at large was protected, even though they were justifying the mental hospital commitment as being for the patient's own good. That segment of the commitment phase was rapidly forgotten once the man was tucked away behind walls. And to complete the sad mosaic, the physician-administrator did not perform according to the tradition of the physician-patient responsibility pattern.

As time went on, however, it became clear to everyone that the mental institution case was, from the legal standpoint, not an ordinary hospital. Ordinary hospitals operate primarily in the realm of the private relationship between the physician and the patient, with decisions being made almost exclusively on the basis of what benefits the patient. In this setting, the court quite properly intervened, in general, only to resolve disputes between the two contracting parties.

In the mental hospital, however, a different situation existed, with the long tradition of incarceration of noncriminal individuals and the extensive intrusion of the needs of society into the decisions which resulted in individuals being deprived of their liberty. The patient, then, was not only but one of *three* parties, but was often at the outset declared unfit to enter into any contract. These peculiar features clearly placed a burden on the court to protect the rights of the individual in this three-way contract. It was most logical, then, that courts would eventually discontinue the immunity the public mental institutions had so long enjoyed.

Once this immunity was set aside, little time was wasted. The neglect and the inequities had been massive and were subject to attack from a variety of quarters.

The Baxtrom case held that a mentally ill prisoner confined to an institution for the criminally insane was, upon completion of his sentence, entitled to civil commitment the same as any other person, with a right to a jury trial under New York law on the issue of his mental illness. The courts demonstrated by this action that even those who had been doubly stigmatized, the "criminal insane," shared basic rights enjoyed by other citizens.

Laws concerning the rights of juveniles, alcoholics, and sexual psychopaths were tested in rapid succession. Adolph Harris, a 16-year-old deaf mute, was placed under the guardianship of the Illinois Department of Children and Family Services on the grounds that he was a "neglected minor." [3] It was found that he had been detained for 430 days in a detention home which had no training or staff for the treatment of people with his defects, and was, therefore, sentenced to a form, a rather bizarre form, of solitary confinement—being a deaf mute. The circuit court found that such confinement did not comport with the statutory premise that the juvenile be afforded "custody, care, and discipline as nearly as possible equivalent to that which should be given by his parents," and that it constituted "cruel and unusual treatment," in violation of the Eighth Amendment. Here was a case where society was saying, "Your parents are doing a bad job treating you and the state will, therefore, take you from your parents and give you the care you should have had." This promise was not delivered and the court, in effect, held society to that promise.

The extension of legal protection to alcoholics was demonstrated in *Easter v. District of Columbia.*[4] In this case, the circuit court of appeals held that *chronic alcoholism* was a defense to a criminal charge of public intoxication and directed that those adjudged as chronic alcoholics be sent to a rehabilitation center rather than to jail. Here was another large number of individuals incarcerated under criminal statutes for a condition which was essentially considered medical in nature. The court displayed a willingness to take a look at this particular practice, disallowing the practice and reinforcing the finding with several other cases involving alcoholics.

These cases, while serving notice that the courts were taking an interest in those who had previously been neglected, were not central in the development of the "right to treatment" concept. More directly in line was the case of *Nason v. Superintendent of Bridgewater State Hospital.*[5] John Nason, charged with murder and found to be incompetent to stand trial, was committed to the Bridgewater State Hospital in Massachusetts. On petition for *habeus corpus,* he urged that the hospital was so understaffed that adequate psychiatric treatment was impossible, and that the standard of treatment at Bridgewater was so inferior to the standards of other hospitals in the state that confinement there denied him equal protection under the law. The Supreme Court of Massachusetts stripped away the therapeutic label and found, through the appointment of a Court Commissioner, that his confinement did not satisfy the promise of treatment. It held that lack of treatment created a substantial risk of violating the due process and equal protection provisions of the Fourteenth Amendment and that, to be sustained as a nonpenal statute, the nonpenal label must have a foundation in fact. In this case, the "right to treatment" concept was actively employed, and demonstrated the court's willingness to utilize such a concept. The issue here was, however, not *adequacy* of treatment, but *comparability* of treatment. Equal protection was the issue, but involved the comparison of how well the promise of treatment was being met in two state institutions.

Another case which presented a logical application of the concept occurred in New York in 1968. In *Whitree v. State*,[6] the claimant was committed to a state hospital after being found "in such a state of insanity that he was incapable of understanding the charge (of assault), or of making his defense." Whitree spent approximately 14 years at Matteawan State Hospital, during which time he allegedly received negligent psychiatric and medical care. After the court examined the record, which showed a lack of both examination and treatment and, incidentally, showed that he was subject to a number of assaults, sexually and otherwise, during his time there. The court, therefore, found it more appropriate to characterize Whitree's claim as a false imprisonment for a substantial part of his confinement. In particular, the court noted that "the lack of psychiatric care was the primary reason for the inordinate length of his incarceration, with the concomitant side effects of physical injury, moral degradation, and mental anguish."

Another factor stressed by the court in its finding was the lack of any hospital record developing information regarding a proposed or existing program of treatment. The court concluded that, "If this man had received proper and adequate psychiatric treatment . . . (he) . . . would have been released from Matteawan State Hospital much sooner."

The action in this case was not to win release, since Whitree had been released. The action in this case was very important and very significant as it was an action seeking damages in tort. Whitree was awarded $300,000 in damages.

The extent of the awakened concern engendered by the emergence of the "right to treatment" issue was demonstrated in a considerably different area. In the 1968 Pennsylvania Legislature, an act was introduced (Pennsylvania Right to Treatment Law of 1968) which not only recognized the right to treatment, but also attempted to create appropriate administrative machinery to assure compliance with the provision of the act. The act died in committee and was reintroduced, but not enacted. The importance here is the "right to treatment" concept has gained enough currency that it is to the point where the legislative interest is being mobilized. A further reflection of the breadth of concern is that the legislative interest was generated through the interests and the lobbying of the AFL-CIO in Pennsylvania.

Probably, the best known case in the "right to treatment" library is that of *Rouse v. Cameron.*[9] Charles Rouse was committed to St. Elizabeth's Hospital in 1962, upon a finding that he was not guilty by reason of insanity of carrying a dangerous weapon, a misdemeanor carrying a maximum sentence of one year. In an effort to obtain his release, he petitioned the U.S. District Court for the District of Columbia alleging that he had received no psychiatric treatment. The Court refused to hear his claim on the grounds that it lacked jurisdiction. On the premise the "purpose of involuntary hospitalization is treatment, not punishment," the D.C. Circuit Court of Appeals reversed, interpreting the District of Columbia Hospitalization of the Mentally Ill Act to require treatment of those found not guilty by reason of insanity. This act had not been directed primarily toward those who had been found criminally insane or not guilty by reason of insanity. It was a civil commitment act which in this case was extended to Rouse.

The court, in this case, squarely faced the issue of "right to treatment" and attempted to provide guidance in the interpretation of this concept, outlining the criteria to be used in determining the adequacy of treatment. It stated:

> The hospital need not show that the treatment will cure or improve him, but only that there is a bona fide effort to do so. This requires the hospital to show that initial and periodic inquiries are made into the needs and conditions of the patient with a view to providing suitable treatment for him, and that the program provided is suited for his particular needs. The effort should be to provide treatment which is adequate in light of present knowledge...the

possibility of better treatment does not necessarily prove that the one provided is unsuitable or inadequate.

Judge David Bazelon, the author of the above opinion, has discussed this issue.[8] He summarizes the intention of the court by stating:

> Ideally, we should be able to ensure that each involuntarily committed patient receives the best and most appropriate treatment. But if psychiatrists cannot agree what this might be in the individual case, it is nevertheless essential to ensure that the patient confined for treatment receives some form of therapy that a respectable sector of the psychiatric profession regards as appropriate—and receives enough of that therapy to make his confinement more than a mockery....
>
> To provide adequate treatment, the critical requirement is that the hospital pay individual attention to each patient and make an individualized effort to help him. There may be gross benchmarks to which a court may look in scrutinizing the adequacy of treatment at a hospital—the ratios of professional and paraprofessional staffs to patients, the physical facilities for treatment, the overall expenditures within the hospital. But there is only one way to measure the treatment provided the individual patient, and that is by the hospital records. If there is an individualized treatment plan created at the inception of treatment and modified as treatment progresses, a reviewing court can hope to assess whether a bona fide effort to provide a meaningful amount of some appropriate form of treatment is being made.

This clarification has crystallized interest in the "right to treatment" issue, causing reactions which have obscured some of the importance of the broader "right to treatment" concept.

The American Psychiatric Association issued a position paper which attempted to provide guidelines for courts and hospitals.[9] Various legal organizations have held symposia such as the one quoted; and, many psychiatric administrators have been looking over their shoulder at this new threat.

Much of this energy is misplaced. First, there have, in fact, been relatively few cases actually involved in this issue and they have been so scattered that any court in a given jurisdiction may agree with Judge Bazelon in his construction and interpretation, or it may not. In a court hearing, in a different jurisdiction, the court may take a considerably different position and hold to a considerably different construction. Each case has, it should also be noted, utilized the concept of "right to treatment" in a somewhat different fashion, making anticipation of future cases even more difficult.

It should be noted, however, that the judicial application of the concept should not, if Judge Bazelon's position statement can, as a practical matter, be used as an example, raise any particular problem within mental institutions which are, in fact, making a bona fide effort for treatment, for the principles he lays down mesh well with the precepts of modern psychiatry. He states that the court will insist that the individual, and efforts to help the individual, must be at the center of any acceptable program. He further states that such must be documented. Neither one of these requirements will conflict in any significant fashion with any hospital which is meaningfully acquainted with modern concepts of psychiatry and modern concepts of medical record keeping.

It should be most apparent, then, that the real significance of the "right to treatment" concept is that it signals, for those with the wisdom to read it, that the basic rights of citizens will be extended into our institutions and that institutional interference in any area of personal liberty will require justification. The administrator of the prison, mental hospital, military service, school, and law enforcement agency must be aware of this basic attitude change and of the need for revision of traditional views and practices. If the view is sustained that unjust detention, abandonment of citizens behind institutional walls, degradation, and dehumanization are, in the long run, far more harmful to society than the release of an individual, practically irrespective of his "dangerousness" or his "undesirability," far-reaching changes will be necesasry.

It seems quite clear that the conspiracy of silence and the failure of vision of society whenever walls are encountered is being shattered and that the abandonment of the inmate by otherwise responsible elements of society is no longer being tolerated. The force of law is being placed behind honesty and against legislative, psychiatric, administrative, or any other societal hypocrisy. The day appears to be arriving when the medico-legal justification "for the good of the individual" must mean exactly that. If confinement is primarily for the good of society, it must be so declared, that that issue can be decided upon its own merits. "Therapy" must *be* therapy—not custodial care, not work performed just to save money for the institution, and not an empty cloak serving only to conceal the operative motives in incarceration. Our jails and prisons, which have been busily hanging out signs proclaiming themselves to be "rehabilitation-oriented facilities" will clearly be called upon to prove it. The hospital in name must prove itself to be a hospital in fact.

## REFERENCES

1. Goodman, Stephen: Right to treatment: The responsibility of the courts. *Georgetown Law Review Symposium, 57:* 1969.
2. Birnbaum, M.: Right to treatment. *American Bar Association Journal,* 46:499, 1960.
3. *In re Harris.* 2 Crim. L. Rep. 2412 Cook County, Illinois. Cir. Ct., Juv. Div., 1967.
4. *Easter v. District of Columbia.* 124 U. S. App. D. C. 33, 361 F. 2d 50: 1966.
5. *Nason v. Supt. Bridgewater State Hosp.* 233 N.E. 2d 908 Mass. 1968.
6. *Whitree v. State.* 56 Misc. 2d 693 290 N.Y.S. 2d 486 Ct. Cl. 1968.
7. *Rouse v. Cameron.* Habeus Corpus No. 287-65 (D.D.C. Nov. 19, 1965), Re'd, 125 U. S. App. D.C. 366, 373 F. 2d 451: 1966.
8. Introduction to Symposium. Right to treatment. *Georgetown Law Review Symposium, 57:* 1969.
9. Position paper on the question of adequacy of treatment. *Am J Psychiatry.* 123: 1458, 1967.

## Chapter 6

# THE STATE GOVERNMENT: PROCESS AND PROGRAM

### Russell Settle, Sr.

Doctor Settle has many years of experience and much exposure with the generally inadequate attempts of states to deal with the mentally disordered offender. He calls upon this background to describe the efforts that some states have made toward dealing with this issue. At the same time, he very persuasively argues that the traditional dichotomy of the mentally disordered offender from other groups is not, perhaps, in the best interest of either the offender or society. He suggests, instead, what he thinks is a more realistic approach to the handling of all individuals who come into contact with our criminal justice system. Lastly, he described in detail new Kansas statutes which he believes represents some forward movement in the direction of improving our traditional approaches to this problem.

EDITORS

I HAVE BEEN ASSIGNED the task of presenting for discussion some of the problems, at the state government level, relating to processes and programs for the mentally disordered offender. Each state is different and no one person can be sufficiently well-informed about many individual state programs to present it adequately. The criminal justice systems; the policies, practices, and procedures; and the governmental climates of the various states are so variable as to add greatly to the complexity of issues which are in themselves intricate and controversial. It is difficult enough to keep focused on the major technical issues, and to avoid becoming entangled in a morass of such legal and psychiatric controversies, without trying to separate out the individual administrative characteristics of the various states. Nevertheless, there is a certain thread of commonality in many of the problems relating to the mentally disordered offender. The legal processes through which these offenders must pass in order to reach a treatment program, and the difficulties of implementing and maintaining effective treatment programs, contain problems which are common to all of us.

I have been an observer of, and, to some extent, a participant in this scene for a good many years. I have long been troubled by what appears to be conflicting conceptualizations, goals which are at odds with each other, and, in general, poor communication and coordination among the various agencies and organizations involved. I have been troubled by the feeling that things are not right, that we are not doing as well as we might, and that there is a tendency to operate at cross purposes. I suspect that these concerns grow out of conflicts between process and program. Many of the problems in the field seem to result from the poor linkage between, and the poor integration of, process and program. Program should flow naturally from process, so I would like to discuss the issues as I see them in this light.

One of the differences between the state governments and the federal government lies in what one might call the phenomenon of dead-endedness. The federal government does not have the responsibility or the authority, except in the District of Columbia, for long-term detention and treatment of chronically disabled, unresponsive, psychotic individuals beyond the expiration of their legal terms; but, under the pressure of *habaes corpus,* such persons, unless specifically adjudicated as dangerous, must be returned to their states of residence. On the other hand, state security hospitals tend to become end-of-the-line institutions, clogged with sizeable groups of chronically ill, more-or-less untreatable and hazardous individuals, with a consequent trend toward custodialism and program inertia. Traditionally, there has just been no place to go from a state security hospital, although the impact of the Baxstrom decision (*Baxstrom v. Herold,* 383 U.S. 107), once its influence is widely felt, may change that state of affairs.

The organizational patterns of state programs for mentally disordered offenders, in spite of variance as to detail, have a lot in common, especially in the smaller states. The larger the state, the more one finds specialized institutions. The smaller the state, the more difficulty it experiences in providing and maintaining humane and effective facilities and programs. I have had the privilege of visiting a number of state programs; and a few years ago collected information from all of the states as to the location and the nature of their facilities and programs, preparatory to publishing a directory. However, The Joint Information Service of the American Psychiatric Association and the National Association for Mental Health pre-empted me in this, and you now have, I'm sure, a copy of their publication entitled *The Mentally Ill Offender*.

The most common state arrangement provides for a security unit, or a building, or a ward, or a section of a mental hospital, operated as a part of that hospital, under the State Department of Mental Hygiene, and designated as the Security Hospital or "C-I Unit." These units serve a number of purposes and mostly house a variety of patients, both from a legal as well as from a clinical point of view. They receive (1) those found by the courts to be not guilty by reason of insanity; (2) those adjudicated by the courts as incompetent to stand trial; (3) sentenced prisoners from the correctional system who have become mentally ill; (4) those patients who are too difficult to control in the regular mental hospitals; (5) "sexually dangerous" persons; (6) mentally retarded offenders; and, (7) in some instances, alcohol and narcotic addiction cases. This hodgepodge of clinical disorders makes for difficult programming, well nigh impossible recruitment of staff, isolation and custodialism, and a reduction of program content to the minimum. Many of these facilities tend to become catchall institutions for referring agencies and courts, which, with all good intentions, believe that they are committing offenders to meaningful psychiatric treatment programs.

The phrase "mentally disordered offender" is, in my opinion, objectionable on several grounds. It cannot be defined, except in terms of some such listing as the seven categories above. Our continued use of it implies that there is some consensus about its meaning, that it constitutes either a clinical or a legal entity. No doubt it came into being for useful reasons, but it allows us to continue to indulge our need to engage in name calling, a propensity from which we need to extricate ourselves. "Legal insanity," "sexual psychopathy," "defective delinquency," "personality disorder," and other similar terms are examples of legal or statutory name calling which were originally presumed to have been mechanisms for matching legal adjudication with clinical needs. Commitments which follow such legal categorizations of offenders result in institutions, or program units, housing patients with such diversity of symptomatology and treatment needs as to make for great program difficulties.

Psychiatric classificatory terminology should probably be purged from the statutes. Its continued use for criminal adjudicatory purposes is not in my judgment in the best interests of society, of the individual offender, or of program development goals. We must search for a better way to meet society's need to protect itself and the offender's need for treatment and rehabilitation. Under the successful "insanity" plea, offenders who are poorly suited for treatment in existing programs too often find their way into mental hospital facilities. The incompetency procedure is too often abused as an expedient, either by prosecutors or defense attorneys who think that they have a weak case and, clinically, "incompetence" is often not a clearly identifiable state; and the diagnosis of sexual psychopathy, as established in a court proceeding, often fails to mesh with clinical indications for psychiatric treatment.

Another objection to the continued use of the phrase "mentally disordered offender" lies in the implication which it perpetuates—that the majority of offenders are not mentally disordered; that is, manifest no psychological disability. No one really believes this, but its program implications are profound. While most, I believe, would concur that offenders generally tend to fall within an etiological continuum, ranging from the socially disadvantaged to those with profound intrapsychic disorganization, we do not intend to imply by this that attention to psychological factors is indicated for only the latter group. It is not necessary to conclude that all offenders are "sick" or mentally disordered, to recognize and advocate that there needs to be a system of classified institutions and community programs, with built-in clinical services, geared to individual needs. But it is doubtful that these needs can best be identified by legal processes or abstract legal definitions, and emphasis on developing treatment programs solely for a group referred to as the "mentally disordered" seems to justify omitting a psychological dimension in programs for other offenders.

Rejection of the mentally ill by the public is by no means a thing of the past. But some progress has been made through educational campaigns, the activities of the National Association for Mental Health and other organizations, and through the impact of federal legislation. Rejection of the ex-convict by society is still the order of the day, even though his acceptance via halfway houses, work release programs, and wider use of probation and parole has opened the door to some extent. But all doors are still shut against those who are both criminal and mentally ill.

Thus, this double stigma, "the mentally disordered offender," is an impediment to progress at several levels. It results in the development of extremely tight custodially oriented bastilles. It gets in the way of probation and community treatment. It makes parole, halfway house, and work release programming less available for these offenders. It impedes staff recruitment because people do not want to work in such institutions. It seems to guarantee low appropriations because of the fear of the mentally disordered offender which the public and legislators have, and because of the hopeless prognosis which clings to such a designation in the public mind and their tendency to "write them off."

We need to be able to demonstrate our effectiveness in treating persons who fall into the mentally disordered offender category, but it's easier to be clear about why we do not do a better job of it, than how to do a better job. As one visits the medium and smaller sized states, one finds relatively small groups of offenders locked away in some confining set of quarters, be it a separate building or simply a ward, where the restriction of movement and lack of access to program facilities are likely to be quite deadening and dehumanizing. Mostly, due to the apprehension and the stigma which carries over simply from their identification as criminal patients, they are denied participation in such activity therapies as the hospital may operate for its other patients. Clinical staff assigned is quite likely to be part-time, having primary identification with other areas of the hospital. The staff then comes to reject and neglect them as being unimportant, untreatable, and surrounded with too many restrictions and hazards to warrant any significant effort. Custodialism and security then take over, with their deadening routines, indifference to individuals, and regressive push. We need to improve our programs for this class of patients, and to reduce some of the public apprehension about them. We need to increase the amount of staff time devoted to them, to look critically at the custodial restrictions which govern their activities, to find ways of involving them more in industrial, educational, occupational, recreational, vocational, religious, and other therapeutically designed activities. We need to do as much as we can to minimize the isolation of these patients within the hospital itself.

I am convinced that one of the greatest impediments to improved treatment programs for mentally disordered offenders lies in this very fact of having set apart a group of persons in mental hospitals as the result of a specific legal process, a specific adjudication, by "hold for court" orders, etc. It is true that there are dangerous and hazardous patients, that each state or each hospital needs a section of greater security. But patients should find their way into such program facilities by virtue of their clinical manifestations and treatment needs rather than by way of some legally arrived at categorization.

I am convinced also that with the increasing barriers to involuntary civil commitment and with the increasing movement toward open hospitals for the treatment of voluntary patients, it becomes increasingly necessary for society to depend on a different process as a way of controlling mentally ill persons who violate the law. If some practitioners had their way, involuntary civil commitments would be outlawed. It would then become necessary to wait until the potentially hazardous patient actually commits a violation of the law before he can be brought under control and treatment. Whether this ever comes to pass or not, it is our experience that our state hospitals generally are becoming less interested in and less capable of dealing with the civilly committed, unmotivated patient, the escape-prone individual, and the hazardous acting-out person who disrupts program and is a threat to staff and other patients. Thus, I see us moving in the direction of fewer offenders diverted to mental hospitals on the grounds of mental illness, fewer having their trials deferred, more use of behavioral science skills after conviction and sentence, and more responsibility on the part of corrections to become therapeutic and provide appropriate treatment for the mentally ill offender, specifically for the offender who is dangerous or hazardous because of mental illness and who requires security management. Mental hospitals have moved far in the direction of less security, and properly so. How far corrections can follow is uncertain, but it should and could move in the direction of more effective treatment within its security settings.

I have no doubt, judging by the institutions with which I am familiar, that there are far more mentally disordered persons already in our major penal institutions than in the so-called security hospitals. Visit almost any state penitentiary and you will find an "adjustment" building, holding from 5 to 10 percent of the institution's population, the majority of whom, the warden will tell you, are mentally disordered persons. He deplores his lack of any meaningful treatment approach for them. The state security hospital, wherever it may be, is full, can accept only limited numbers, and in desperation the harassed prison medical staff is prescribing tranquilizers by the bucketsful. It is apparent that the current, much wider use of probation is changing the nature of penal institution populations, by screening off the most stable and best adjusted offenders for community treatment and sending the most disturbed to corrections. There can be no argument with this approach, but it is apparent that recognition must be given to this changing population, to this changing role for corrections through support of expanding comprehensiveness of program.

I conclude from this, however, that our legal "processing" is a failure. Even if we are dedicated, which I am not, to a process which purports to separate the "bad" from the "sick," at the court level, it is evident that we are doing a very poor job of it. If it worked properly, we would not find the so-called "mentally disordered offender" in penal institutions. Among other reasons, it does not work because it is based on the premise that mental disorder is a static condition which can be identified on the basis of legal definitions. It is here, in my judgment, that the breakdown between process and program is most evident. How can effective program development be expected to flow from a process which purports to identify the mentally disordered offender and then does not do it? It seems to me that we must go one way or the other and agree that all offenders are "disordered" and should be under the mental health system or that all law violators are appropriately subject to the correctional process. You might counter by pointing out that since the system already allows large numbers of mentally disordered offenders to enter the correctional system, and asking, Why hasn't corrections done a better job of treating them? Could it be, in part at least, because the goal of the criminal justice system is punishment, euphemistically called protection of society? Society's message to corrections, via the criminal courts, is to the effect that the courts will identify the sick, send them to hospitals for treatment until they are recovered sufficiently to be tried and punished, and that corrections need not really concern itself about mental disorder or abnormality. Is it too surprising then that corrections has not made more progress in treating the mentally disordered offender?

Surely, the legal profession and the courts can help us find a way out of this impasse. It is easy to advocate abolition of the plea of insanity, but very difficult to bring it about, although abolition of the death penalty might go a long way toward placing it in limbo. Surely, a legal processing system can be found which addresses itself only to identifying the offender and his offense and arranging for his most appropriate treatment, instead of fruitless preoccupation with separating the punishable from the unpunishable, and the competent from the incompetent. Surely, we can now abandon the concept of punishment in favor of control and treatment. Surely, processes which focus on dangerousness, need for control, and rehabilitative potential, are now rational, in keeping with the present state of behavioral science knowledge, and favorable to the promotion of law and order and good correctional programming. How long do we have to live with the myth that a mentally disordered person may not be sent to a correctional program, when we know that it happens constantly? How long do we have to live with that famous contradiction "not guilty by reason of insanity?"

Such queries and concerns, of course, are not new. They are admittedly not very practical. We are not likely to change profoundly or easily the ways in which the judicial process deals with mental illness as it relates to criminal behavior. We are not likely to be able to shift quickly the emphasis of the criminal justice system from punishment to treatment. We have to live with reality, with things as they are, even while devoting some of our energies to working toward change.

I believe that we have made some change, some slight forward progress in the area of process in my own State of Kansas. On July 1, 1970, Kansas placed in operation a revised criminal code and a revised code of criminal procedure, both of which I believe contain some provisions which enhance the capacity of the judicial process to respond to the mental illness factor in criminal behavior. Most of the details of these lengthy documents, which required years of study and work to develop, are not pertinent to the considerations of this Institute. There are some points, however, which are of interest:

First, the new Kansas Penal Code follows the general idea of the Model Penal Code in that all crimes are now grouped according to their severity, each group having its own flexible minimum sentence to be set by the court within specific limits, and an established inflexible maximum.

Secondly, all specific references to psychiatric categories have been removed. There is no sexual psychopath, defective delinquent statute, or provision for criminal commitment for drug or alcohol addiction.

Third, after conviction, but before sentence, the court may defer sentence indefinitely pending examination and/or treatment in any public or private institution with suitable custody and program. This allows for great flexibility in responding to the case in which mental illness or disorder has been identified, be it psychopathy, addiction, or psychosis. The offender may not be involuntarily detained, however, longer than the maximum sentence for the offense.

Fourth, after sentence, commitment is made to the director of the correctional system, who is given great latitude in allowing sentence to be served in any public institution with suitable program and custody. Thus, the need for special care and treatment may be met through completely flexible program arrangements suitable to the circumstances in individual cases.

Fifth, the procedures for obtaining psychiatric appraisal of competence to stand trial are made quite flexible so as to fit the circumstances of individual situations. The court may order psychiatric examination at a community mental health center, by an individual psychiatrist, or by a commission of two physicians while the subject is in jail or on pretrial release; or by commitment to a state hospital, the State Security Hospital, or to a private institution. It is made clear that a hearing must be held and that the determination of competence to stand trial is a matter for judicial decision.

Sixth, those adjudged incompetent to stand trial must be committed for treatment to a state, county, or private institution. Time spent in such treatment in a public institution is to be credited against any future sentence. Parole is authorized if subject does not recover competence but is suitable for community release and the court approves.

Seventh, no statutory definition of criminal responsibility was adopted. Defendant must declare his intention to so plead thirty days in advance and must agree to abide by the orders of the court regarding arrangements for examination.

Lastly, those found not guilty be reason of insanity must still be committed to the State Security Hospital, whose Director has the power of convalescent leave or discharge thirty days after notice is given to the sheriff and county attorney.

These amended procedures appear to complement the already existing provisions in Kansas for the evaluation of convicted felons after sentence and commitment to the Penal System. The Kansas Reception and Diagnostic Center, a unit of the Penal System, conducts a full-scale psychiatric, social, educational, and vocational evaluation of all persons committed to the custody of the director, up to the limit of its capacity. These evaluations and treatment recommendations are intended primarily for the use of the institutions in the Penal System for program planning purposes. Reevaluations are done for the Board of Probation and Parole, in selected cases, at the time parole is under consideration. The initial reports are also available to the sentencing court, which retains jurisdiction over the offender for 120 days, and may, within that time, set aside the sentence, place the offender on probation, send him elsewhere for treatment, or place him in a community program.

While these changed procedures are in no sense any final answer to the problems being considered at this Institute, it is expected that by providing greater flexibility they can promote the development of better programs for those referred to as "mentally disordered offenders." Certainly, such programs do not now exist in Kansas in sufficient quality or quantity. But these statutes lessen the urgency of separating the "sick" from the "bad" in the judicial process by establishing more flexible ways of providing treatment before trial, after conviction, before sentence, and after sentence. Hopefully, we can now proceed to establish improved capability to provide such treatment.

It seems clear to me that these, and similar statutory provisions in other states, are but patchwork attempts to make existing legal processes more responsive to program goals. Commendable as they are, they do not reach to the basic discord between process and program.

I suggest that improvement in the care and treatment of the mentally disordered offender is inextricably linked to the expanded utilization of behavioral science knowledge and psychological insights in all of corrections, and that our specific objectives for the mentally disordered offender should be as follows:

First, we must seek alterations in the judicial process which focus it more exclusively on the identification of the offender, shift the role of the clinician from pretrial evaluation to post-trial treatment, and at least abate the adversarial preoccupation with psychological issues and legal definitions. The legal profession should be urged to work with us in finding such altered procedures even if it means that every offender be held accountable for his acts, at least in some measure. This would not be inconsistent with the psychiatric approach to the treatment of the individual patients.

Secondly, we must unequivocally support the doctrine that all persons charged with a crime are entitled to their day in court, and that only the severest degrees of mental disorganization justify its postponement. An educational campaign among the medical and legal professions is needed to emphasize that incompetence to stand trial is a legal, not a medical, concept; that it is not the equivalent of mental illness; that it should be regarded as a temporary state until proved otherwise; that it should be adjudicated only in the presence of profound disorganization; and that in borderline cases the doubt should be resolved in favor of the accused's right to prompt trial.

Third, vast improvement of correctional services must occur. Corrections must develop comprehensive programs of treatment, as well as control, for all offenders, including the mentally disordered offender, embracing the total range of community-based as well as institutional services. The professions, particularly Medicine and the Law, have failed thus far to speak up and lend their not inconsiderable weight in support of increased staff, improved facilities, and enlightened programming for those who violate the law.

And, fourth, perhaps our greatest need is for increased skills and knowledge. The professions must speak up loudly and clearly in support of the search for new knowledge, the better implementation of that which currently exists, and the search for altered statutory procedures which will make the criminal process more responsive to the needs of society and the offender. It is only through greatly augmented behavioral research and a climate of academic inquiry, training and experimentation that we can attract the necessary clinical personnel into the correctional system. The time is at hand for funding prospects are now better than ever before through the provisions of the Omnibus Crime Control and Safe Streets Act.

I have presented a point of view with which many others will not agree, but I suspect that not much progress will be made until we have reconciled our different points of view, insofar as that is possible, and have agreed upon a strategy which we can all support. The April 1970 Report of the President's Task Force on Prisoner Rehabilitation repeatedly emphasizes its recommendation "of diverting as many defendants as possible from the full criminal process." However, I cannot help but seriously question the practice of the easy pretrial diversion of defendants into mental hospitals. I do not believe, by and large, that the mental hospital of today is the answer to providing appropriate care and treatment for hazardous, socially deviant, acting out behavior. Hospitals are moving in a different direction. If your experience is like mine, admission to a regular state mental hospital in such circumstances very rarely results in any substantial gain. The hospitals do not want them, they are not motivated to become involved in hospital programs, and runaways and further offenses are frequent. Furthermore, if the criminal process is that bad, that unresponsive to social concerns, as it may well be, we ought to change it rather than circumvent it.

Progress, in my judgment, clearly lies in the direction of giving the responsibility for the mentally disordered offender to the correctional system and demanding that it meet it responsibly.

## Chapter 7

# THE FEDERAL GOVERNMENT: PROCESS AND PROGRAM

### Pasquale Ciccone

As Director of the United States Medical Center for Federal Prisoners, Doctor Ciccone is uniquely qualified to describe the federal statutes regulating the medical, surgical, and psychiatric care provided for all persons charged with or convicted of a federal offense. In addition, he details the programmatic operation of that facility as it relates to psychiatric care of both groups. The facility at Springfield, Missouri receives only the more seriously disturbed individuals within the federal system. The program in operation there is an attempt to involve the total staff in an integrated and system-wide approach that will maximize the offender's early return to the sending institution.

EDITORS

I PLAN TO focus the discussion on the treatment of the mentally disordered offender from the perspective of the role of the Medical Center for Federal Prisoners, Springfield, Missouri. The mission of this institution is to provide intensive medical, surgical, and psychiatric care to all offenders charged or convicted of a federal offense who are physically in the custody of the U.S. Attorney General and accomplishing such care in the framework of a safe and secure penal institution. In effect, therefore, the Medical Center acts as a service institution for some 30 major institutions and, now many smaller facilities such as the Community Treatment Centers and county jails housing federal offenders. In addition, the Medical Center provides diagnostic services at the request of the Federal Courts throughout the nation, including care of mentally disturbed, or the so-called criminally insane individuals, adjudicated as incompetent to face charges by the federal courts.

The diagnostic services provided to mentally disturbed offenders have been in effect over a period of only 20 years. The statute relating to consideration of competency is Chapter 313 of the U.S. Code, Title 18, Section 4241 through 4248, enacted by Congress in 1948 and 1949. The federal law governing the disposition of the mentally ill persons who are charged with or convicted of offenses against the United States, briefly summarized as it exists today, is as follows:

1. Title 18, U.S. Code, Section 4241. This section authorizes a Board of Examiners at each penal institution to report to the Attorney General when a prisoner under sentence is found to be mentally ill. Such an inmate is transferred to the Medical Center where he is to remain until restored to sanity or until maximum sentence without good time allowances is served. (Section 4243 authorizes the Director of the Medical Center to transfer the mentally ill prisoner to the proper authorities in his state of residence at the expiration of his sentence.)

2. Title 18, U.S. Code, Section 4244. This section, along with Section 4246, is the heart of Chapter 313. Section 4244 provides that whenever the U.S. Attorney has reason to believe the accused in a criminal proceeding is insane or otherwise so mentally incompetent as to be unable to understand the proceedings or properly assist in his defense, he shall move for a determination of mental competency setting forth the grounds for his belief. The motion may also be made on behalf of the accused or by the court. Upon such motion, the court shall cause the accused to be examined by at least one qualified psychiatrist who shall report to the court. The court may commit the accused for a reasonable period to a suitable hospital or other facility for the examination. The hosiptal so designated is frequently the Medical Center for Federal Prisoners, Springfield, Missouri. At present, we are receiving from 20 to 25 such cases a month from judicial districts throughout the United States with orders to conduct such an examination. The court must hold a pretrial hearing and make a finding with respect to the issue of competency.

3. Title 18, U.S. Code, Section 4245. This section relates to a post-conviction determination by physicians concurred in by the Director of the Bureau of Prisons that the inmate was probably incompetent at the time of his trial and the issue was not raised. Upon such a determination, the prisoner is returned to court for a hearing similar to that authorized by Section 4244. If the court finds that

the prisoner was incompetent at the time of trial, it shall vacate the sentence.

4. Title 18, U.S. Code, Sections 4246 and 4247. If the accused is found to be mentally incompetent, Section 4246 provides that the court may commit him to the custody of the Attorney General until he is competent to stand trial or until disposition is made of the pending charges. Under Section 4247, the court may also determine whether the accused will probably endanger the officers, property, or interests of the United States if he is released. If these conditions exist, his commitment is to run until he will no longer endanger such officers, property, or interests, or his competency is restored, or his care and custody is assured by his state of residence whichever event occurs first.

At this point, I would call attention to the fact that there are no provisions in the U.S. Code for a federal civil commitment. Nor are there any provisions for the commitment of a defendant who has been acquitted solely on the ground that his mental condition at the time of the alleged criminal conduct precluded criminal responsibility.

Since the enactment of Chapter 313, Title 18, U.S. Code, Sections 4244 and 4246, there has been a gradual increase in the use of the facilities of the Medical Center for individuals confined under these sections. At the present time, there are generally from 30 to 40 individuals who are confined at the Medical Center under Section 4244 and from 90 to 100 who are confined under Section 4246. The decision as to whether the accused should be confined or examined on an outpatient basis is a matter for the court's discretion. Section 4244 provides that the trial court may order a competency examination to take place at a suitable hospital or other facility. However, no statutory provisions relate to procedures to be followed when the examination is conducted locally, and no authority exists for the use of Veterans Administration, Defense Department, or Public Health Service facility for competency examinations. Since these facilities are normally unavailable, an accused is frequently transported long distances for a competency examination. Thus, they may be transported from California, Florida, or New York to the Medical Center in order to undergo such examination. Studies indicate that the duration of an average Section 4244 commitment to the Medical Center is approximately 60 to 90 days. A number of problems arise out of such confinement for Section 4244 examinations, namely it is costly to the government and prejudicial to the accused. The accused is denied the opportunity for pretrial release on bail or personal recognizance. He is also removed from family and counsel while his trial is delayed over several months, or even indefinitely if he is subsequently found incompetent. In recognition of such consequences, both the criminal division and the Federal Bureau of Prisons have suggested to the courts that whenever possible, Section 4244 examinations should be conducted on a local outpatient basis. A revision of Chapter 313 is under consideration and this should make clear that local outpatient examinations are to be ordered in all but the exceptional cases in which examining psychiatrists show cause for prolonged confinement.

The Medical Center is the only institution under the authority of the Attorney General with the facilities to treat persons who are incompetent to stand trial, in other words, Section 4246 commitments. Consequently, such persons are of necessity treated in much the same manner as those who are under sentence. Until recently, these individuals, unsentenced prisoners, were totally commingled with the sentenced prisoners. That is to say, they were housed in the same dormitories as well as participating in all other programs of the institution together with sentenced prisoners. Very recently, we developed at least a token separation by housing unconvicted individuals in a separate building. However, they still participate with sentenced prisoners in almost all other programs of the institution, such as common eating facilities, educational facilities, recreational facilities, and the like. There are a few differences in the handling of the unsentenced prisoner and the sentenced prisoner. The differences chiefly are that unsentenced prisoners may work on a voluntary basis only. Courts have ruled that we cannot subject unconvicted persons to involuntary servitude. Another difference in the handling of unconvicted prisoners under Sections 4244 or 4246 is the almost unlimited mail and visitor privileges. We do inspect mail for contraband in the interest of maintaining safety and security of the institution, but we do not restrict the correspondence list, nor in any way censor the writings of such individuals. Under the present structure, there is a fairly well-formulated psychiatric treatment plan for the group of unsentenced prisoners at the Medical Center. There are three physicians responsible for providing the necessary services with the assistance of a social worker and a nurse. In addition to handling the routine medical problems, the physicians are responsible for the psychiatric evaluation of all court cases and, upon subpoena, testify in courts throughout the country. They participate either directly or in a consultant capacity with the group counseling community meetings, group therapy meetings, and group socialization meetings. All of this is part of the regular treatment program involving a treatment team approach with the doctor, nurse, social worker, and correctional officers, all members of the treatment team.

The policy at the Medical Center is to return the accused to court within a reasonable period of time. In the case of Section 4244 commitments, the average stay is 60 to 90 days. In the case of Section 4246 commitments, a study completed several years ago indicated that over 10 percent of the incompetency population at the Medical Center had been confined for over three years. The longest commitment at that time was for 97 months. Administrative efforts have been made to shorten the stay. However, there are many problems. First, in many cases of this kind, the accused has no state of residence or his state of residence is not willing to commit him under civil proceedings. Since the federal government has no civil commitment statute, it has no authority to confine these inmates aside from Sections 4246 and 4247. Therefore, when it appears that an accused is not fit to be released from custody, either because of his disability or dangerousness, charges are left pending for long periods of time under the theory that the man may some day return to trial. In other cases, state authorities may be willing to initiate civil commitment proceedings, but the U.S. Attorney for the trial court in the prosecuting district will not, for one reason or another, dismiss charges. Finally, some inmates have been sent to court as competent in the viewpoint of the psychiatrist, but they have been returned following a contrary judicial determination. There is presently no statute of limitations for the trial of persons found incompetent and attacks on confinement on the basis of the Sixth Amendment, guarantee of a speedy trial, have failed. The policy generally at the Medical Center is sensitive to the accused's right to a speedy trial. The accused is reevaluated by the institution three months after his original commitment and every six months thereafter, unless the court requests more frequent reports. When the accused has been at the Medical Center for a sufficient period of time that the psychiatrist is convinced that the prognosis is bleak, and certainly no longer than 15 to 18 months, the institution recommends dismissal of charges and state hospitalization. Judication of competency is the role of the court. The psychiatrist's role is that of an expert witness to inform the court of the results of his tests and studies of the accused and relate how these results bear upon the issue of competency.

The above discussion has addressed itself to the process as well as to the procedures as it affects the accused, mentally disturbed individual, who has not been convicted by the court. The remainder of my discussion will relate to the psychiatric program for the convicted, mentally disturbed offender. These individuals are referred to the Medical Center either by designation from the central office, directly from courts, or from other institutions after having been found to be insane by a Board of Examiners, whereupon it is mandatory that he be referred to the Medical Center. Or as it more frequently happens, the referring institution requests admission of an individual whom they have found to be mentally disturbed without the formality of a Board of Examiners. The criteria for referral to the Medical Center is that an individual is referred for psychiatric evaluation because of certain bizarre behavior which requires such evaluation, or it has been determined that the patient requires psychiatric treatment not available at the referring institution, or it is determined that there is a need for psychiatric control and facilities for such control are not available at the referring institution. These mentally disturbed inmates are transferred from any of the institutions within the federal penal system to the Medical Center and treated with the objective of restoring them to an improved state of mental health so that they can be referred back to their originating institution where the "corrective processes" can be more meaningful.

The psychiatric program for convicted mentally disturbed inmates at the Medical Center was recently restructured in accordance with a treatment program that was developed by our staff psychiatrist.

Actually, this program has been in effect for less than six months. In addition to the use of psychotropic medication as indicated, and crisis therapy when indicated, there is a plan of treatment tailored to the needs of the patient as required by his behavior. All sentenced psychiatric patients are housed in one building known as Ten-Building which is divided into different units which lend themselves to a physical structure that can facilitate treatment of groups of patients with similar needs. Every patient in this complex has an individual room. The doors to each room can be opened or closed in accordance with the level of progress in the mental status of the patient. Each unit varies in the degree of control exercised on the unit from the most maximum of security to a level of minimal supervision for those patients who are able to accept community responsibility. The general direction is to develop a climate consistent with a therapeutic community approach, and the entire treatment program is carried out by a treatment team consisting of the physician, the nurse, the social worker, and the unit officers assisted by participating psychiatric consultants. The treatment team handles the total care of the patient while he is at the Medical Center. The chairman of the team is the doctor. The social worker has the responsibility for organizing the dockets and arranging for patients to be present. The various teams meet once a week and review the patients in order to develop a plan of treatment and to discuss progress. This is done with the patient being present. In addition, each unit has a community meeting once a week which lasts for one hour. This includes all the patients on that unit and the members of the treatment team. Additionally, each community is subdivided into groups of eight which meets at least once a week and engages in a therapeutic encounter. Each group has a leader, who is a professional staff member, and a co-leader who is a correctional officer. For the past several years, we have been engaged in training lay staff in counseling techniques so that they can be an extension of the professional staff in creating a therapeutic climate. There are three staff psychiatrists assigned to the total psychiatric program for sentenced prisoners. In addition to the above responsibilities of participating in community, group, and team meetings, the doctors have the responsibility of evaluating each sentenced patient within 24 hours after his arrival and also seeing the patients on his caseload for sick call, crisis therapy, and individual therapy if this is needed.

Patients are housed in progressive units in accordance with behavior. Patients treated on the intensive treatment unit consist primarily of three types: (1) acutely psychotic patients who are so withdrawn and disorganized that they cannot function around other people; (2) suicidal patients who require observation and the opportunity to be under less stressful situations; and, (3) chronically assaultive patients. All treatment in the intensive treatment psychiatric unit is on an individual basis and no set rules are made for treating patients as a group, but rather treating them as individuals. Each officer working in this unit is assigned a number of patients with whom he works on a one-to-one basis. If he so desires and has compatible patients, he can work with them in small groups. Patients are given a radio, reading material, medication as needed, a minimum of 30 minutes of contact with the officer who is responsible for him, in addition to the contacts for necessities such as daily meals, medication, and the like. Various programs are added as the patient can tolerate them such as television under supervision, card games, meals with others at a picnic table inside the unit, occupational therapy, and supervised yard privileges. When the patient's mental status has improved so that he can tolerate other people, he immediately is moved to the next unit where a similar program is in progress with the addition that the patient becomes involved in more group therapy and has much more contact with other people in the unit. Again, when the patient has made sufficient improvement, he is transferred to what is known as the work release unit where the program is expanded to include eating with the rest of the population and going out to work at various locations in the institution, but other institutional activities are restricted. He is given a trial in this unit for two to four weeks and if he can make it in this unit, then he is moved to the next more advanced psychiatric unit where the patient becomes involved in the total institutional program.

A complex of three similar units constitute the next progression as the mental status of the patient improves. Each of these units contain 48 individual rooms, each with a commode and wash bowl in the room. On each unit, there is a large day room which is used for television viewing. There are two smaller rooms, one on the lower level, used for ping-pong and games, and the one on the upper level used as a quiet reading room. The doors to all rooms are kept open from six in the morning until ten at night on each of these units. There are no gates closed between the units, and the patients can visit together from the different units during the day. Visiting in each other's room is not permitted, but free interaction between patients is permissible in the halls and in the day rooms. The program is built around the treatment team interacting with the patients, as previously described, including the individual and group work performed by the staff psychiatrist, the nurse, the social worker, and especially the unit officer with community meetings, group therapy, and group socialization meetings as previously described. Patients in these units are encouraged to participate in the total institutional program which includes work assignments, education, recreation, religion, and various other kinds of activity, such as Alcoholics Anonymous, Gavel Club, Black history and culture studies, Bible studies, and the like.

There are two additional units that complete the complex that make up the psychiatric service for sentenced prisoners. One unit is a special unit that includes individuals characterized as characterological manipulators. Because of their peculiar propensities, a degree of control, insofar as the physical restrictions are concerned, is maintained. Individuals in this unit do eat with the rest of the population, participate in work, and the rest of the total institutional program. Community and group meetings held by this group are indeed interesting to observe since their manipulative characteristics are especially obvious in the meetings and it becomes intensely interesting to see one manipulator attempting to manipulate another manipulator. The other unit is the most permissive unit in terms of the therapeutic community where a great deal of responsibility for living in this community is placed upon the individual. This unit generally includes the most improved psychiatric patients or the cases where it is thought that they have a particular need for this kind of exposure.

The above description is but an overview of the psychiatric program as it presently operates at the Medical Center for Federal Prisoners, Springfield, Missouri. Each institution within the federal penal system has a hospital and may have a mental health program. Presently, there are approximately 21,000 federal offenders incarcerated in federal penal institutions. Our statistics show that approximately 10 percent of this population exhibits a degree of mental disturbance that requires some form of treatment. We do not have sufficient beds at the Medical Center to care for this population. Our total psychiatric beds at the present time consist of 280 beds for sentenced mentally disturbed offenders and 140 beds for the unsentenced mentally disturbed offenders. Therefore, obviously, a goodly number of the mentally disturbed within the federal penal system do require some kind of mental health program in their respective institutions where they happen to be incarcerated. At Springfield, we receive only the more seriously mentally disturbed offenders.

The objective at the Medical Center is to develop a program involving the total staff. At the present time, the staff is augmented by graduate students from the University of Missouri, a number of volunteers from the community, and a number of undergraduate students from local colleges who spend several hours each week under staff guidance taking practicum work for college credits. This cadre at the present time is 25 to 30 people who come at various times during the week. The basis of our treatment depends upon the impact of people on people. Of course, as a penal institution, we do have to maintain security. However, our staff are impressed with the fact that their main responsibility is treatment and that good treatment is good security. We have opened many doors. Although the structure of the institution's psychiatric program that I have described is a relatively recent development at the Medical Center, we think that the results have already begun to demonstrate that significant improvements can be anticipated. The program is being watched by our staff with enthusiasm. We are beginning to return our patients to their original institutions at a much faster rate than previously and the expectancy for even better results is high.

## Chapter 8

# THE THERAPEUTIC COMMUNITY IN A MAXIMUM SECURITY HOSPITAL–TREATMENT IMPLICATIONS

### Roger S. Kiger, M.D.

The maximum security hospital presents considerable challenges in developing a meaningful treatment program. Doctor Kiger has spent the past 11 years at the Maximum Security Unit, Utah State Hospital refining the therapeutic community milieu that functions there. His paper describes their program in these areas: (1) hospital organization; (2) therapeutic community milieu; and, (3) treatment processes. Doctor Kiger indicates considerable enthusiasm for the utility of the therapeutic community, and makes many practical suggestions for dealing with the sociopath so frequently found in maximum security settings. Some problems with maintaining a therapeutic community are identified and discussed.

EDITORS

IN AN EFFORT to do justice to the monumental subject matter contained in the topic at hand, I have organized this presentation into three broad sections: (1) hospital organization; (2) therapeutic community milieu; and, (3) treatment processes. A functional therapeutic community cannot exist and prosper without adequate implementation of these three basic areas under consideration and you will note that each blends with the other. The content of this preparation is primarily derived from 11 years experience of living with the Maximum Security Unit treatment program at Utah State Hospital, Provo. Understandably, the material will be presented in thumbnail fashion but hopefully with enough principle to provide fruitful stimulation. Those who are interested in more detail or elaboration may resort to the references listed.

## HOSPITAL ORGANIZATION

All public mental institutions in the past, and many at present, have been characterized by a fairly rigid hierarchial structure. The organization has been oriented to the needs of the system rather than to the needs of the patients. In this setting, interprofessional rivalries and friction were propagated by departmentalization, each specialty claiming superior therapeutic potential. Everyone assumed that what he was planning was for the good of the patient—but the patients were rarely consulted. In fact, each individual and group was controlled in one way or another, and new ideas were frowned on because of the effect they might have on the organized setup. Therapeutic efforts were fragmented because there was no cohesive, unifying force within the system, and personnel often acted at cross purposes.[1] In 1957 and 1958, some state hospitals, particularly in the western half of the country, began reorganizing according to the principle of decentralization or the unit plan.[2, 3] Simply stated, decentralization involves the dividing of a large hospital into several autonomous units, usually to serve specific geographic areas. This makes it more possible to clarify the chain of responsibility by abolishing dual lines of authority and to eliminate ambiguity about who is responsible to whom and ideally allowing each employee to be responsible to only one other person. Besides developing a better treatment community within the hospital, the unit plan should merge with the concept of offering total care, including precare and aftercare, which extends efforts into the surrounding community.

Important factors in determining the process of decentralization for a given hospital include personnel and personalities, number of patients, the physical facility, finances, community attitudes and culture, politics, and so forth. Difficulties in reorganizing are to be expected and should be dealt with as they appear. Personnel are threatened because of various factors such as change itself, the existence of atrophied positions and functions, rigidity of personalities, and exposure of incompetence. Everyone has to get closer necessitating more communications, both formal and informal, with everyone else. This is a very painful change for some people whose social skills and particular kind of interpersonal skills have actually atrophied through disuse in the traditional organization. It is a very significant role change and has been threatening to many people. Some feel stripped naked of the kinds of defenses, protections, and barriers that have been erected by and for themselves by virtue of the structure of the institution. This ranges from the psychiatric aide who no longer finds it possible to hide under the cloak of menial tasks to that of the administrator, who must become familiar firsthand with unit processes by participating and getting his feet dirty in the fields rather than sitting behind his desk, overseeing the plantation. In their new roles, staff members must relate to one another and to patients in many ways that were not dreamed of before.[4]

In a renowned case of failure on attempting to decentralize, the clinical director stated that the move was made too fast, there was much resistance from old-guard employees, and there was not enough support from the administration. He added that under the traditional custodial system the hospital had areas labeled intensive, chronic, untidy, or disturbed. After changing to the unit plan it had, instead, intensive psychiatrists, chronic psychologists, untidy nurses, and disturbed administrators.[5] It is highly desirable for the administrator, whether on a superintendent or team leader level, to possess ingredients of patience in permitting the seeds planted to germinate and grow, the permissiveness that allows employees to use initiative and be responsible for their actions; yet the firmness and expectations that demand results.

The advantages realized in successful reorganization far outnumber and overbalance the difficulties encountered. The completed process affords continuity of therapeutic efforts because patients are always treated by the same team instead of being shifted from one group of personnel to another. By the same token, treatment can be consistent because responsibility can be accurately assigned. The staff functions as a team instead of a chaotic assembly of individuals, each marching to his own music. Communication between staff and patients is easier, because the treatment team has common goals, responsibilities, and identifications; feedback is more reliable, meaningful, and significant. There is no argument about decisions, because the decision-makers are the ones who do the job. More flexibility is present, providing that staff members and patients are given realistic opportunity for creative thought and independent activity. With decentralization, we can realistically expect more from staff members and patients. People, as we know, tend to respond to environment and to other people's expectations of them. This response is apparent in a maturing unit team, and new leaders constantly develop in the ranks.[2]

I have alluded to mental hospitals in general regarding the processes of proper organization. Let it be emphasized that no where is such needed more than in a maximum security hospital setting or on a maximum security unit within a given institution. Each hospital, of course, because of its particular set of circumstances will have to decide the type of organizational setup it can best function with. There are those who have implemented a flow type of system or some other modification of the unit plan utilized. This may well work for some; but for the most part I believe that the desired goals are made more difficult and the culture media achieved is less conducive to a therapeutic community milieu. Some of the inherent handicaps include less heterogeneity of patient constellation, more likelihood of passing the buck syndrome from one ward or unit to the other, less need for staff incentive to develop new techniques and sophistication outside their "specialty," and scattering of energies when each team is not dealing consistently with a designated catchment area and its community representatives. Taking a critical look for violation of principles in organization and mode of operation is indicated when a facility is experiencing undue difficulties.

## THERAPEUTIC COMMUNITY MILIEU

Once a hospital is organized properly and functioning on an efficient level, the foundation has been laid for the development of a therapeutic community. In most treatment units, however, the professional staff are sitting in ivory towers ordering, prescribing, and directing. The patient is planning, demanding, manipulating, and using individuals and groups against each other. Other associated people, such as psychiatric aides or relatives, are in the middle—not knowing where they stand or how to function effectively. They identify unhealthily either with the patient or with the treatment staff. In such a situation there are three worlds, contemporary but unrelated, with the patient in control of an anti-therapeutic milieu.

Brifly stated, the "Therapeutic Community" is a social matrix that affords the opportunity for people to use their initiative and ability in dealing with their problems through therapeutic processes. This includes everyone involved; the couch is no longer reserved just for the patient. The five basic principles necessary for the fulfillment of such a milieu have been stated by Maxwell Jones, M.D. They are (1) bilateral communication; (2) confrontation; (3) decision making by consensus; (4) multiple leadership; and, (5) operation of living-learning groups. The essence of these ingredients cannot be overemphasized and will become more than apparent as the presentation unfolds. The term "Therapeutic Community" has become a household word within our circle the past few years, and unfortunately it has been used as such by various psychiatric facilities. Some have modified traditional treatment concepts a bit, instituted a few innovative procedures, or implemented some of the more recent "mod" type group processes and publicly announced that they now have a therapeutic community. Others have made more sincere efforts but have fallen short for one reason or another such as lack of understanding, limited resources, or not being willing to put forth the energy, inventiveness, and fortitude required. In spite of well-laid plans and a potentially good media for developing a therapeutic community, difficulties may still be encountered and progress appears to be lagging. When this happens, it is usually due to people; and those people are usually staff members rather than patients. In my experience, patients are much more resilient and amenable to change with the expectations required than are staff. No doubt some of this has to do with the fact that most patients never are completely contented with the treatment program available and almost any suggestion for change is greeted with a hopeful attitude.

The treatment team's role is vital in the therapeutic community milieu and consideration has to be given to blurring of roles required, personalities involved, cohesive performance of its members, and other aspects of functioning referred to throughout the paper. I am not too concerned about the team size as long as there is adequate representation of the disciplines and skills required and as long as there are enough people to get the job done. The designated leader plays a key role in determining the functioning and character of a given community. Needless to say, influences seep throughout the total community as determined by the caliber of standards and norms established through the leader's enthusiasm, beliefs, integrity, drives, and acceptance of his own mistakes. This does not mean the team leader's role should be an authoritarian one; in fact, such is contraindicated. Naturally, there are clear-cut lines of authority within the team if one takes the trouble to find them, but less thought and energy should go into demonstrating "who's boss" than into producing ideas to solve a problem.

Heterogeneity of patient composition can be a decided asset as compared with a homogeneous setting created by segregating different types of patients. The latter setting is conducive to reinforcing the "birds of a feather" type of functioning with psychotic and "honor among thieves" type of behavior with the character disordered. The ward rules and structure which usually result is a message for the patient to behave as expected; namely, to continue in a psychotic fashion or act out as not being responsible. In my experience, admitting acutely disturbed or behavior problem patients to an adequately functioning community is preferable to a separate admission ward. Older patients seem to be able to understand the psychotic's dilemma in such a way as to reassure him and absorb some of the agitation and fears present. Likewise, the con-artist displaying negative or aberrant behavior is confronted with a bevy of experts who have played the same game. In a heterogeneous setting, many sociopaths will identify with and have feelings for some of the less fortunate patients or the "underdog" and the value is obvious. A change in attitude is often seen when he is allowed to work with a regressed patient and has been able to promote some degree of improvement in him—particularly when the staff have been unsuccessful for years. Conversly, the apparent dichotomy of a regressed patient being able to say and point out things a sociopath has a blind spot for has marked impact. The successful integration of the sexes with living arrangements on the same ward for the past seven years has been one of the most potent and useful tools at the writer's disposal.[6, 7] Unfortunately, treatment teams in some facilities may have to work without the benefit of this advantageous circumstance.

Although staff role and heterogeneity are important, the basic foundation for the development of a therapeutic community is an active, functioning, and democratic patient government in conjunction with various group processes all of which include and involve patients. Patient government should not exist in name only; nor should it function under the guise of a "Mickey Mouse" project. The officers should be elected by the patients according to their well-defined constitution, articles, and bylaws. The process of patient involvement should extend into every facet of the unit team functioning. The program in our unit allows for patient representation during scheduled staff meetings and "postmortem" sessions following community meetings. Patients, likewise, do not exclude staff during daily patient council and ward meetings. Psychiatric aides are assigned as consultants with various processes of patient govermment including buddy groups, recreation committee, the patient posse, orientation committee, housekeeping group, personal appearance committee, doorwatch responsibilities, and special treatment programs with individual patients. Other procedures tied in with patient government and the therapeutic community include suicide watch by patients, fire drill exercises, staff personnel and patients eating together, the unit baseball team, patient of the month plaque, and designation of a patient coordinator whose responsibility it is to assess and submit a weekly report on the functioning of ward organizational processes.

I believe that the patient having a voice and being actively involved in the overall treatment program is one of the most important principles that pertains to a therapeutic community. He is the potential key team member and the real expert in knowledge of needs and modes of procedure within his immediate environment. Our faith in his ability to make decisions and be responsible for them is an important factor in harnessing this potential. It can be anticipated that one problem will be the resistance of patients to tell or "rat" on one another. There will always be those who say, "If you don't tell on me, I won't tell on you and we can both get what we want." This attitude can be overcome and they can be convinced that relating information will help others when such material is brought into the open and discussed. Patients have to learn to appropriately identify with and feel for one another, understand each other's problems, and thereby be of aid to all in helping. This means giving him considerable responsibility, and the staff has to function in a democratic way rather than in an authoritarian fashion.[1]

The community meeting is one of the best settings in which to instill therapeutic principles and to facilitate their development. It should be the heart of any therapeutic community program, should involve everyone concerned, and should be ruled by majority vote. In this setting the group can continually explore, accept, modify, or reject ideas in an effort to come up with better ways of functioning. Goals should be set rather high and every effort made to maintain them. The community meeting should become a problem-solving group, discussing all things pertaining to a patient, a ward, or a unit-wide problem. This body can discuss role relationships, point out process problems, discuss therapeutic goals for individual patients, train staff and patients in group techniques and personality dynamics, make decisions, and set unit policies.

This type of group setting when blended with the total treatment program brings about the following positive processes:

1. Each member of the community has more responsibility in terms of his individual problem and/or role, the problem of others, and overall community involvement.

2. Better communication enables everyone, regardless of his position, to react in a more consistent fashion to a particular patient or problem. Being a part of the discussion and decision-making engenders confidence in members who become involved in subsequent treatment processes.

3. Teaching and research are greatly enriched, especially when each community meeting is followed by an intensive postmortem. Ideas are constantly worked over to fit specific situations, and they are presented on the spot to everyone present. Thus the teaching process has a dynamic, meaningful quality often lacking in a classroom lecture where people are removed by time and space from the ongoing processes.

4. Patients become therapists instead of passive recipients of therapy. They are able to more effectively learn and exert the principles of peer confrontation than is possible in other settings.

5. There is a minimum of authoritarian pressure and a maximum of peer pressure which is conducive towards utilizing the assets and potential of the sociopath.

6. Staff-patient relationships are enhanced. One example is that

of staff being less often pestered by requests when they walk onto the wards. Patients become less dependent on individual staff members and more dependent on the problem, one another, and eventually themselves. They no longer see staff as a jailer to be manipulated or an authority to be justifiably defied. Staff members, in turn, become more a part of the total team effort and mutually cooperative endeavors.

In developing a therapeutic community milieu, it is important for appropriate subgroups and/or the total community to handle undue incidents in a stepping-stone fashion. This usually takes the form of certain procedures being added whereby people and processes mature rather than becoming frustrated and threatened. An extremely important prerequisite, especially with the embryonic program, is that a solid foundation exists on which each step is based before extending the program into little known and unexplored spaces. Through observance of this common-sense rule, the community is in a better position to develop new techniques and procedures with which to work.

## TREATMENT PROCESSES

Obviously, many aspects of patient and staff involvement have necessarily been included in the material thus far presented. There is a need, however, for elaboration while considering treatment processes. This section will, therefore, concern itself with three subdivisions—patient participation, staff role, and observations. The focus will be centered primarily on principles in treating the sociopath. It is sometimes forgotten that Dr. Maxwell Jones's therapeutic community was first developed for those with behavior problems. All maximum security hospitals and units have more than their share of the offender who is characterologically disordered. If this element is not handled appropriately, the best conceivable program will be torpedoed forthwith. On the other hand, proper utilization of the sociopath's characteristics and channeling of his assets can result in his contributing immeasurably to treatment processes. Contrary to traditional concepts, treatment of the sociopath can be successful and my experience has led me to believe that he responds better than do some alcoholics, long-term schizophrenics, obsessive-compulsive neurotics, and those with various other personality disorders. Patients who fall into those classifications do not usually have enough of the sociopath's positive qualities.[6] Indeed, society in general profits considerably from the stimulation afforded and contributions made by our rogues who are able to function short of breaking the law. It should also be stressed that the processes of treatment ascribed to are applicable to most psychotic patients, particularly the paranoid. The reality-oriented approach and therapeutic endeavors are geared towards the needs of maladjusted people rather than diagnostic labels. Whether psychotic or sociopathic, their basic needs are the same; their psychopathology is similar—the major difference is in their symptomatology or behavior.

## Patient Participation

In the successful therapeutic community, patients are active in participation with fundamental processes such as expectations, confrontation, peer pressure, and placing high value on privileges that have been earned by assuming responsibility. In this milieu it is socially acceptable for an individual to be psychotic, but patients generally have little tolerance for a peer who misbehaved particularly when his actions have an adverse effect on their well-being. In one well-remembered case, it was finally decided after heated discussion in a community meeting that a sociopath of questionable motivation and integrity be given a grounds pass. One qualification consisted of the patients laying their privileges on the line for the trusted one, should he betray the group's confidence and discredit the community. When he eloped a short time later, the patients closed the ward and suspended valued activities as allowed by their constitution. During the lull, patients and designated staff members spent their time constructively by pinpointing weaknesses and evaluating everyone in an effort to upgrade the functioning of identified individuals and the program as a whole. When the offender returned he was dramatically confronted with the effect his irresponsible action had on others, but with little result. Finally, his best buddy volunteered to go into seclusion for him until such time as he was willing to respond to the satisfaction of the group. This not only made it possible for the offending patient to remain physically available for confrontation by his peers, but it also placed him in an embarrassing position that made his familiar defense reactions useless. Through this experience he finally began to recognize and respect the rights of others and he started to behave more appropriately. Patients often deal more strictly with their fellowman than staff members and the sociopath more readily accepts that disciplinary measure than he would a lesser penalty demanded by authority.

Patients being allowed to assume responsibility is not only an important treatment process but is a cherished one. This is a relatively new experience for the sociopath because the authority he flouts usually reacts by rejecting and punishing him; that response, of course, triggers his negative feelings and offensive actions against society. The development of a patient posse is a case in point; this places responsibility for policing the patient where it clearly belongs—on the patients themselves.[8] Its primary functioning has to do with preventive measures and escorting services, but it also deals with elopements, fires, and other emergencies. It should be a self-perpetuating and highly organized group with inauguration of such procedures as liaison with hospital security personnel, possession of identification cards, screening and grouping of patient activities whereby each watches the other, requisition of walkie-talkies, development of teams for geographic coverage in cases of elopement, facilitation of standby transportation, working agreement with local law enforcement agencies, and enhancing relationships with local townspeople. One of our more dangerous patients was under a criminal charge of kidnapping. He forced his way out of the hospital by overpowering a psychiatric aide, but the patient posse returned him to our custody. In spite of public alarm during the interim, the outcome resulted in a favorable report in the local paper. A year later, the newspaper reported that the same patient had, in turn, been responsible for returning another escapee to the hospital under similar circumstances. The therapeutic efforts for all concerned were immeasurable. Since the establishment of the patient posse eight years ago, only one member has taken advantage of his position of responsibility by eloping while on duty.

Often positive results are seen by allowing a patient responsibility for a project that has a definite relationship with his own problem; hence, an individual adept in thwarting the law might be a prime candidate for posse chairman or open door watch. As we know the sociopath is a master at wrongdoing and manipulating and is, therefore, adept in spotting another's techniques. Although he may use poor judgment in examining his own behavior, he is usually quick to detect the same behavior in others. Many potential culprits can be "converted" and planned escapades can be nipped in the bud by the patient's zealousness to protect his own comfort and hard-earned privileges. Taken further, most will develop a desire for making the program a success. One useful procedure is to create an atmosphere of challenge against great odds. Nothing will rally the sociopath to a cause more effectively than the chance of putting something over on authority. With our proposal to have open doors and plate glass instead of locks and bars, higher authority who might disapprove were taken into consideration. In such a process, patients usually ally themselves with staff and generally learn to compromise, tolerate frustrations, develop a better set of values and gain the satisfaction of accomplishing something worthwhile.

## Staff Role

Many of the sociopath's characteristics usually considered therapeutically detrimental can often be used to achieve positive treatment results. The therapist should always keep in mind, both glaring and subtly, expressed characteristics which tie in with the treatment approach in a dynamic way. The more pertinent ingredients are those of feelings towards authority, the way he relates with others, demanding and taking much but giving little, the apparent lack of sense of responsibility, best adjusting to the situation he controls, blaming others for his plight, flight from anxiety, distorted self-image with feelings of inadequacy and lack of self-esteem yet seemingly satisfied with himself, and a tendency towards aggressiveness with a need for instant gratification.[6] Some of these ingredients and related treatment processes have been covered but additional comment is necessary.

Therapists have to be firm and realistic in approach, yet warm and understanding in demeanor. The message to be conveyed is that while a staff member likes the patient as a person, he cannot condone untoward behavior. Expectations have to be set rather high about the performance of everyone in the treatment process, including staff;

undue permissiveness allows the patient to be disillusioned and disbelieving of those dealing with him. Staff honesty is vital, and honesty is something to which the sociopath is unaccustomed because of the type of interchange he usually experiences with other people. Some may express anger at direct and honest confrontation, but will at the same time experience a strong feeling of respect for the authority figure. Belief in the patient and in the program is a basic ingredient in any therapeutic milieu; if staff members hold this belief genuinely and demonstrate it realistically, the sociopath will be more inclined to consider the common goal. While it is essential to relate with him during the processes involved in the treatment program, personal and emotional relationships should be avoided. Moreover, it is well known that patients entering a treatment setting are inclined to identify with certain personality types whereby the interpersonal relationships are parallel with those of previous significant people. This pathological interplay should be recognized early and dealt with appropriately. One male sociopath was quite successful in perpetuating his pattern of behavior and obtaining rejection by exposing himself while in seclusion. The resultant problem, as related to some female personnel, was beginning to overshadow the primary issue. Many people spent considerable time in attempting to deal with the ramifications that developed—all to the patient's delight. This dilemma was "miraculousy" solved in a moment of simple but rare insight on the part of a hospital aide. When confronted with the sociopath's weapon, she merely said, "That looks mighty interesting, but isn't it awfully small?" Since manifest behavior is the result of previous reinforcement, it naturally follows that inappropriate behavior can be ignored or rejected and acceptable behavior reinforced. The essence of this primary learning principle seems to escape some therapists. It is appalling to note the relatively high rate of communication that actually reinforces pathological behavior.

In pathological transference and counter-transference situations, especially with the refractory patient, behavior modification techniques of one type or another can prove to be quite useful. Such a modality ties in well with the therapeutic principle we have called "instant therapy." This can be effectively implemented by staff and peers in treating the more primitive, immature, demanding, and acting-out sociopath. Usually, strict discipline over a considerable period of time has been unsuccessful. The patient continues to demonstrate impulsivity, aggressiveness, and disdain for authority with an inability to learn from experience wherein behavior demonstrated five minutes earlier is only of passing historical interest. This individual has to be confronted with his behavior immediately and appropriate action taken at once if it is to be effective. There is a need to discuss the basic principles on experiencing such an episode and draw-up appropriate negative and positive responses to the behavior expressed. The value of this approach is inherent through its simplicity, frequency of application, and involvement of the peer group as well as the receiver.[9]

Setting appropriate limits is imperative. They are better tolerated if everyone involved has a voice, but staff needs to keep certain fundamentals in mind. Few limits should be set because the sociopath resents numerous restrictions and busy personnel cannot keep track; when some are overlooked, the overall intent becomes impotent. Limits should be clearly defined because vagueness and ambiguity lead to a different interpretation by everyone; staff becomes frustrated and the sociopath finds reason for a sense of injustice. Limits have to be realistic if they are to be effective rather than patients playing games with them; in fact, they usually encourage unrealistic limits. Prompt enforcement is essential and if not adhered to is likely to lead to further acting-out. Moreover, personnel see no point for the rule and everyone develops feelings. Sound reasons have to be given for every limitation; it is surprising how many times the wrong reason is given for the right restriction.[10]

Occasionally, staff should make changes in the program in order to maintain some unpredictability. That serves to prevent processes from becoming too routine which causes the sociopath to lose his enthusiasm and fall back into his old patterns of behavior. In a well-functioning therapeutic community, however, most patients' actions soon became common knowledge. The kicks the sociopath usually gets through his manipulations and undermining efforts are lost because his behavior is exposed. This results in pressure from others, and typically the sociopath follows the most comfortable path because it is less anxiety-producing. Rather than buck the community, he will become part of it. Despite his initial ulterior motives, he becomes involved with the ongoing processes in a more positive fashion. It helps in dealing with the complexities involved if the therapist has just the right touch of the sociopath's own characteristics; levers can be beneficial or detrimental depending on who is holding the handle.

Perhaps the most pertinent treatment process staff can foster is the nonverbal message patients receive. Placing them in the setting described, for instance, demonstrates more clearly than words that we not only believe they can behave like responsible people, but it is expected of them. I have observed that sociopaths can indeed learn more satisfactory patterns of behavior and better ways of functioning if they are repeatedly exposed to new, careful designed experiences. Apparently, the underlying pathological forces are modified if one can appease his basic need to feel more secure, independent, responsible, and self-composed, and when we can enable him to develop self-esteem through a sense of achievement.

## OBSERVATIONS

Maintaining a program of this type for a meaningful period of time is considerably more difficult than developing one. The reasons are many, but some of the more significant will be mentioned. A perennial problem is the high rate of turnover of patients and loss of key personnel. New members have no vested interest in the processes, but inherit what has been accomplished by the hard work and efforts of those who preceded them. The inexperienced therapist and those with certain types of personalities are threatened by the procedures involved. There is naked exposure to the scrutiny of sharp-eyed patient observations and some professionals may think that they are losing their rightful control. It is imperative for the team leader to keep on top of the situation by constantly pinpointing potential problem areas and mandatory for him to continually teach and preach about seemingly well-known procedures and principles.

As inferred, the amount of energy required is demanding. Staff rationalization that a successful therapeutic community has no more goals to strive for is associated with a loss of ambition for further accomplishment. The diminished enthusiasm inevitably seeps throughout the ranks and results in deterioration of treatment processes. Such can be one of many causes for a weakening therapeutic community.

Some signs of this syndrome include vague communications with less information being submitted and more requests being made, superficial community meetings and patients playing patsy in their overall functioning, anxiety of staff members, personality clashes and clique formations, acting-out with more seclusions being resorted to, an atmosphere of fear on the ward, and regression of the more sick patients. When these earmarks become manifest, the underlying factors have to be assessed and handled.

Crises of varied types can lead to dire consequences particularly if the therapeutic community has not been realistic and has over-extended its capabilities. On the other hand, crises should be turned into therapeutic assets by developing better treatment procedures and innovative group processes as a result of the situation. It helps, of course, to have a good relationship with the public and news media. One way to enhance this is by the utilization of a patient panel which presents the program to the local and state community through public appearances of various types.

Some people think the treatment concept presented gives the patients too much responsibility. It must be stressed that the professional staff, by giving patients more responsibility, do not abdicate their own. That is one of the most important therapeutic procedures involved. Delegating appropriate responsibility to patients leads to processes that give even more responsibility to staff. It is a gray area. Where does the responsibility of the patients end and that of the staff begin? In some obvious cases, no clarification is needed, but in others there may be more subtle considerations. My experience shows that the continuing processes result in an unspoken agreement about where those lines are drawn. Some patients, of course, are continually probing and testing, usually manifesting the problem that brought them to the hospital in the first place. Staff must recognize when such testing is taking place and when it is handled appropriately, a therapeutic experience results. Nor should the philosophy described be construed as being overly permissive. On the contrary, the community should expect responsible behavior in return for privileges, and tremendous pressure is placed on everyone to work for future responsibilities and privileges.

In conclusion, the need for better understanding and more appropriate treatment of the mentally disordered offender becomes doubly important now that the incidence of character disorders is increasing out of proportion to the population explosion; society is busily concocting a culture that is an excellent breeding medium. No given treatment program should serve as a blue print, but hopefully the fundamentals ascribed to in this presentation will be of value to others. Whatever you model, may it be one that has feet which do not contain too much clay, is endowed with keen vision which allows for perception beyond the facades exposed to, contains the heart to heed the anguished cry of the sick, has a head which is able to come up with better ways of handling the mentally ill than in the past, and possesses a backbone which will be able to hold up under the tremendous load required.

## REFERENCES

1. Kiger, Roger S.: New programs solve old problems. *Ment Hosp, 15:* 657, 1964.
2. Kiger, Roger S.: Adopting the unit plan: I. processes. *Hosp Community Psychiatry, 17:*207, 1966.
3. Heninger, Owen P.: Adopting the unit plan: II. perspectives. *Hosp Community Psychiatry, 17:*211, 1966.
4. Pepper, Max P.: Decentralized state hospitals—an overview, *A Critical Review of Treatment Progress in a State Hospital Reorganized Towards the Community Served.* Colorado, Pueblo Association for Mental Health, 1963.
5. Garcia-Bunuel, Leonardo: The Clarinda decentralization experiment, *The Organization of the Hospital for Optimal Patient Care.* Colorado, Western Interstate Commission for Higher Education, 1962.
6. Kiger, Roger S.: Treating the psychopathic patient in a therapeutic community. *Hosp Community Psychiatry, 18:*191, 1967.
7. Peterson, C. Leslie and Kiger, Roger S.: An open security ward. *Ment Hyg, 51:*223, 1967.
8. Patients of South Salt Lake Unit. Bird's eye view of our posse. Paper presented at Institute on Therapeutic Community Development & Implementation, Utah State Hospital, February 5-7, 1970.
9. Andrus, R. S.: Instant therapy in a ward community. *Hosp Community Psychiatry, 17:*147, 1966.
10. McDonald, J. M.: Acting out. *Arch Gen Psychiatry, 13:* 439, 1965.

# Chapter 9

# ATTITUDE THERAPY

### James C. Folsom

Attitude Therapy was developed as a patient management technique at the Menninger Clinic in the late 1920's. It is used extensively in many mental health facilities throughout the country. One of the most active proponents of this technique is Doctor Folsom. He has written and lectured extensively on this topic, and the Veterans Administration Hospital at Tuscaloosa, Alabama has been widely cited as a model in the application of Attitude Therapy. In this paper, Doctor Folsom describes some of his personal experiences which formed his opinions about what can and cannot be done in a mental health facility. Doctor Folsom concludes his paper by discussing some of the basic Principles of Attitude Therapy.

Editors

Earlier in the Institute, Dr. Karl Menninger was referred to as "an angry old man." I come to you now as "an angry middle-aged man" because I think there are some things to which we ought to address ourselves. I take no issure with what anyone else has said, but I wish to present my point of view.

I was reared in a Methodist preacher's family so, at a very early age, I knew a lot about heaven and hell. Some time ago, I spent the day in what must be as close to Hell as there can be on this earth. This was in a mental hospital in south Alabama, formerly all Black, with 2500 patients crowded into an area adequate for approximately 1000. I saw patients sitting on backless benches all day long. When I asked one of them how he spent his time, the reply was, "I just sit." And I said, "Well, do you leave the ward ever?" He replied, "I goes to meals." I asked him what time and he didn't know. It was as if time had no meaning for him. He asked the psychiatric aide, who was more of a guard than anything else, and learned that he went to breakfast at 6:30 A.M. I asked the patient what happened to him after breakfast. "Well, I come back to the ward and I sits."

I asked, "How long do you sit?" "Ah, till it's time to go to dinner." "Well, what time is dinner?" Again, he didn't know. He asked the aide because I wouldn't. I wanted this to be his involvement. He learned that he went to lunch at 11:00 A.M. He was back on the ward at 11:30 A.M. and then he sat. And he sat on the backless bench till 3:30 P.M. when he went to supper. Then he returned to the ward and sat until bedtime.

There were 160 patients on the ward. This was the story of the lives of all but ten of the patients. These ten, I learned, were allowed to leave the ward. Six worked at the chicken house and four worked at the barn. They were the lucky ones. They were allowed to leave the ward. There were patients sitting, staring, waiting out an eternity.

I visited the 200 criminally insane in the same hospital, on that same day. I saw an adequate number of guards standing around. I felt absolutely safe on the ward. I think I would have been willing to stay the night not fearing that anyone would hurt me because I had never seen such a sterling example of behavior modification. Their behavior had been so shaped that they no longer had a spirit of their own. They were doing nothing. They were making no decisions. On this ward of 200 patients, only four were doing anything meaningful. The others were sitting.

All the patients were sitting on backless benches. Of the four who were involved in an activity, one was writing a letter. I questioned him. He was writing his mother. Two older patients were playing checkers on a board that was drawn on the bench between them. They were straddling the bench with the board between them. One young patient, who had recently been transferred from the state hospital in the northern part of the state, was watching television. Would you believe it, the hospital official escorting me turned off the television set. I asked him to turn it on again. He responded, "Well, it's too noisy." I said, "Well, at least he's doing something. Please, for me, would you turn it back on?" Since I was a guest and he was showing me around, he turned it on again.

I went to observe the serving of meals. I saw 100 patients in a room, one single room, seated on backless benches. There were two rows of beds lined up behind the rows of benches on each side. The patients sat all day. Some were so infirm that they were tied to chairs and some were in wheelchairs. When it came time to feed them, they were handed trays that did not look too clean. Some other patients came in pushing food in stainless steel containers. The patients lined up for their food. The patient doing the serving walked the hall with a big container and slopped the food onto the trays. Following him was someone with a macaroni dish served in the same way. Then someone else placed large pieces of cornbread on the trays. Finally, someone else served the applesauce. That was the meal. It was slopped all over the floor. I was almost to the point of vomiting by the time I was able to leave the building. I came away from that one day visit physically sick from what I had seen.

I happen to believe that a great deal can be done about things like that. Until that time, there had never been a woman on the men's side of the hospital. There are now female nurses assigned to the male wards. The superintendent, who really was a fine person and through the years did the best he could with very limited finances, retired recently at the age of 74. The new superintendent, who is in his mid 30's, is doing an outstanding job.

I visited other wards where patients were mutilating themselves. One woman was able to bite her breast to the point that she would get hunks of flesh out. She had also bitten her arm until it was a mass of scars. The suggested solution was to pull all of her teeth. Fortunately, her teeth were not extracted. I had agreed to serve as a consultant for one day. However, I was so distressed by what I saw that I thought, as a native of the State of Alabama, that I should do something about it. I agreed to go back a day and a half each month.

The operating budget was approximately six dollars a day per patient. There was no increase in funds and personnel. In spite of these drawbacks, a miracle occurred at that hospital. Previously, orderlies and nursing assistants were not listened to and they functioned only as guards. Their job was to deliver the patients, either individually or in groups, to the psychologist or social worker in their office. Now they are members of the treatment team. Incidentally, the psychologist and social worker rarely communicated with one another. It was as though there was an imaginary line down the middle of the hallway. It was never crossed verbally, nonverbally, or physically. This has been changed. Their offices are now on the wards.

Other amazing changes have occurred. The nurse, who was formerly not allowed to do anything but pass out medications, took it upon herself to buy material to put up drapes. She took sheets home and dyed them gold to match the drapes. On the ward, where there had been no activities at all, the nursing assistants, *as team members,* now have an extremely active arts and crafts program.

What does it take to change a situation like this? I maintain that it's people who make other people mentally ill. I think that it takes people to treat mental illness and I believe that mental illness can be treated.

I would like to speak just a moment about my ideas of medication. I want to tell you about an experience in another state hospital. I spent some time in a mental health institution in the early 1960's. I received a telephone call one evening from a nurse on duty saying that the medical officer on duty would not order medication for a disturbed patient. He said it was the fault of the new program that the patient was disturbed. One of the most dangerous patients on the ward, one feared by everyone, was quite upset. Although it was against my own regulations to give an order by telephone, I gave her a prescription for one of the strongest medications.

There happened to be about eight inches of newly fallen snow on the ground. The snow plows were out but I did not want to risk that road even though I had snow tires. I said, "I really shouldn't come, if you just have to have me, I will. But I would like for you to try this and then if I don't hear back from you I will assume that everything's okay." I was told that the chart would be on my desk the next morning for me to sign the order. When I arrived at my office the next morning, the chart was on my desk. I signed the order and sent it back to the ward.

About two hours later, the chief nurse walked into my office. She placed a chart in front of me. It was the chart with the order to be signed for the medication. I said, "But, Miss, I've already signed the order." She said, "Well, I was hoping you would be so busy you wouldn't even ask me anything, but we had a nursing error. The medication was given to the wrong patient. So you have to sign it here on the chart of the patient who actually got it."

Now the moral of this story is that it really was not that patient who needed the medication, it was the staff who needed it. They needed something to give them the strength to be able to handle a situation that was getting to almost riot stages. They were able to handle it by the magic of some liquid in a syringe pushed through a needle into the flesh of a fellow human being, who just happened to be a mental patient.

I had other experiences there that convinced me that drugs often get credit for changes when in reality other factors are responsible. A patient, hospitalized for 30 years, was placed on a special ward where drug therapy was a major part of treatment. She made very nice progress in the drug program. She had been doing extremely well and she was on privileges for the first time in many years.

A series of articles appeared in the paper about the cost of the mental health program. The high cost of drugs was specifically mentioned and the costs of individual drugs were listed. This patient came by my office and indicated that she wanted to see me. She had come by to talk with me on several occasions and I always profited by her communications. She had learned much in 34 years of hospitalization about how *not* to treat human beings. She said, "I'm afraid they'll lock me up again." I said, "Why is that? Aren't you getting along well? We're making plans now for your discharge." She replied, "Yeah. But if I tell you the truth, you'll probably lock me up again." I said, "I'll promise you, for telling the truth you won't be locked up again. So what is this truth?" She said, "Well, I read the paper over the weekend and I've really been worried about it. I didn't realize that these drugs were so expensive." After a pause she continued, "They put me on this drug ward program about 18 months ago, but I have never swallowed a pill. And I hate to waste it this way. And since I found out how much it cost, I just can't go on gyping the government this way." She was not locked up. The drug order was stopped. Soon after this episode, she was able to move into the community.

I admit that these are two isolated examples, but still I hope my point is getting across. I do not believe that drugs are all important. I believe that *people* are important. It's the way people are used that is of utmost importance.

I liked the statement I heard by another speaker, "Good treatment is good security." I agree with this statement. If you have a good treatment program and if you have a program that not only your staff can believe in, but that your patients can also believe, then you will have a program that encourages security and progress. There is just no way for you *not* to make progress.

In 1962, after two years in the program I have just described, I returned to the Veterans Administration. When I assumed my new position as chief of staff, my secretary handed me a list to sign. I said, "Well, what is this list?" She replied, "This is the pass list for the weekend." There were about 20 names on the list. I didn't know any of the patients. I had met some patients. I had been to some meetings where patients were discussed, but none of the 20 on the list. I said, "I can't sign the list." She replied, "Oh, you have to sign the list or otherwise they can't go on pass." My reply was, "It's not proper for me to make this decision about who can go on pass. I know nothing of their behavior. I don't know if it's in their best interest to go on pass. I'm in favor of passes, but we've got to get this changed."

So I called the staff together and asked, "Whose decision should it be?" "Well," everybody said, "the ward doctor." We discussed this issue. It was pointed out that the ward physician did not know how the patients were behaving most of the time. We looked further into the problem. Someone asked, "How about the nurse?" After more discussion, we decided that the nurse was not around that much either. Maybe it should be the aide. Then we decided, "No, the aide doesn't really know. It's the patient who really knows whether he ought to go on pass, could profit by a pass." So we changed the procedure. Instead of the list being compiled by the nurse with the concurrence of the doctor and sent to me for signing, the patients placed their own names on the pass list. Then there was a group discussion with the patients and staff present to see whether or not they should have their passes.

For years, doctors made the decision about the amount of security the patients needed. However, the physician really knew the least about it. He was not there at night. He did not know what patients he could really trust and what their behavior meant. Therefore, we made this procedure a team decision. One that is made with the concurrence of the patients.

Presently, we have patient operated wards. The criminally insane ward previously described now has only a population of 54 instead of 200. The ward is lively and jumping. They have a badminton set with the net stretched across the day room. They have a nude, life-size poster of Jane Fonda behind the door in the conference room. It's a bit distracting. They have patients from the criminal ward working in the Patient Operated Program. All decisions are made by the patients. They also assist with the feeding of the blind patients. The ward where they were "sloppen' 'em like hogs," now serves patients cafeteria style with no increase in personnel. It's simply a difference in the feeling about the worth of a human being. This is the only thing that's changed.

The concept of attitude therapy and the team approach have also been introduced at that facility. However, they cannot be credited with the changes that occurred. What is responsible is having personnel free to do what they are capable of doing and giving them the responsibility to do it.

## ATTITUDE THERAPY

Attitude Therapy was developed at the Menninger Clinic between the years of 1925 and 1930. It is a management device. I see it as good creative management. It's getting the job done. It's getting everyone in on the act; as active participants in an ongoing process. The Menninger Clinic found that some patients did not respond as well as they thought they should. Being the group that they were, they took a real hard look at both their successes and their failures. They decided that the biggest problem was the lack of consistency. In other words, they believed that they were repeating some of the inconsistencies that had originally led to the formation of illnesses in their patients. Incidentally, I do not hold to the biological theories of mental illness. As I see it, people make people sick. I am not concerned about genes and biological theories. I do not believe that we should just put chemical restraints on all of our patients until some knight in shining armor comes riding upon his white charger with the magic cure. I think we already have the cure for mental illness—people who care and know how to use themselves therapeutically.

What we now call Attitude Therapy was developed over a ten-year-period at the Menninger Clinic. A general description of that technic is best presented by quoting from an in-house publication of theirs first drafted in 1935 and revised in 1950.

> These (the general attitudes) are extremely important since, if we are to accomplish the therapeutic aim, it is essential that all persons who come in contact with the patient should maintain a uniform attitude insofar as possible; in other words, one nurse must not be 'indulgent' and another 'severe,' or one therapist must not be 'solicitous' and another 'indifferent.' Since the system of treatment for the patient is based on contact with many different members of the professional staff, it can function well only when everyone with whom the patient may come into contact maintains the same general attitude toward him. Furthermore, the attitude assumed toward a patient is probably more important than any particular activity. There is reason to believe that the manner in which we say things and the atmosphere created through our attitude is actually more important than what we say and what we do. Many patients react to our feelings and manners much more than they do to our words.

I believe that Attitude Therapy is a further refinement of milieu therapy, in which patterns of maladaptive behavior are identified and proper attitudes prescribed. Attitude Therapy enables the individual to change his behavior and develop self-determination. The training of paraprofessionals to work with this technique is stressed.

A treatment team may prescribe one of five attitudes: (1) Kind Firmness, (2) Active Friendliness, (3) No Demand, (4) Passive Friendliness, and (5) Matter of Fact. Some therapists are so skillful that they can treat five patients with five different attitudes at the same time, if it is indicated. However, not all staff are capable of utilizing all five attitudes.

### Kind Firmness

Kind Firmness is that treatment attitude of taking over completely for the depressed patient, allowing him to make no decisions and assigning him to nongratifying work during all of his waking hours. We have not used electroshock treatment at our hospital since 1963.

Let me tell you about a research study that we did. We wanted to assess the effectiveness of an antidepression program which, in our clinical judgment, was superior to the ego-supportive therapy so widely in use. We wanted to compare antidepression program with the Kind Firmness Attitude with the Active Friendliness Attitude.

The antidepression program provides a depressed patient with a highly structured environment in which every staff member coming into contact with him applies the Attitude of Kind Firmness. The depressed patient is put in a small, rather drab room furnished with chairs, table, and a few shelves where a monotonous task is assigned to him. The task may consist of sanding a small block of wood, bouncing a ball, counting little sea shells and putting them in a cigar box, mopping the floors, making beds, and other such menial tasks. These assignments provide physical activity and focus his attention. He is never given anything to do that will bring him gratification.

Kind Firmness Attitude indicates that all staff working with the patient are to insist that he carry out all tasks assigned no matter how much he may complain. Staff are not to give in to his pleadings to be left alone to suffer. They are not to try to cheer him nor to offer him sympathy and encouragement. In fact, speech by the patient is discouraged. The patient is kept under close supervision at all times with a small group of other depressed patients. He is allowed no visitors, no mail, and no telephone calls. All tasks are assigned by nursing assistants to assume a level of expectancy approaching perfection. Any shortcomings in the patient's performance are pointed out to him. In the case of a patient who is severely depressed, it may be necessary for the nursing assistants to take him by the hand and assist him to sand the block of wood. The patients in this program are kept busy all their waking hours, except during meals and hourly breaks. If they do not sleep at night, the work program is continued. It should be emphasized that while the patient's performance is criticized, he, as a person, is never ridiculed or belittled.

The purpose of this program is to provide an opportunity and cause for the expression of hostility. After there has been an appropriate externalization of his anger, the patient is taken off the program. Patients are usually cured of their depressions in three to five days. So it is not nearly so long as one would think. I would also like to point out that what we are trying to do is to take a psychoanalytic approach. We believe that the patient has introjected an ambivalently held love object and now he has to get rid of it because the hate part is in him and he has to kill himself. If you prefer the operant conditioning or the learning theory models, he has learned to get his attention and his kicks by looking for sympathy in being depressed. As the individual slows down psychologically and physiologically, depression takes hold and he is no longer in control of himself. We believe the antidepression program, combining the Kind Firmness Attitude with a boring work program, reverses this process.

Now for the opposite attitude used in the research.

### Active Friendliness

This attitude is considered by the staff to be at the other end of the continuum from the Attitude of Kind Firmness. It requires that all staff members be actively friendly with the patient no matter how personally distasteful he may be in his personal habits, in his language, in his physical appearance, or in any other personal qualities. This requires that the staff move in and take over for the patient through total involvement. The staff is supportive and through personal assistance do not allow him to fail. They are building successes for him. This approach provides a safe and friendly setting in which he receives praise as an immediate reward for his accomplishments. This approach has previously been known as TLC, tender loving care, or giving love unsolicited. In such an environment the patient can again become involved in activities and social interactions, a diminishing fear or failure he has been so accustomed to experiencing. This attitude is prescribed for the apathetic, withdrawn, noninvolved individuals; frequently regressed and deteriorated chronic schizophrenics.

Subjects were selected for this study from newly admitted patients who presented depression as a major symptom. Patients who could not complete the research battery of psychological tests were excluded. Patients were selected without regard to diagnosis or type of depression and were randomly assigned to six groups: Kind Firmness only, Kind Firmness with placebo, Kind Firmness with antidepression medication, Active Friendliness only, Active Friendliness with placebo, and Active Friendliness with antidepressant medication. The research battery of psychological tests consisted of the MMPI, the Tennessee

Interpersonal Check List, and the Department of Mental Health Concept Scale. This battery was presented (1) prior to commencing treatment; (2) two weeks later; (3) six weeks after initial testing or at the time of discharge, whatever came sooner; and, (4) a follow-up administered six months after the date of commencing treatment. There were 86 patients distributed among the diagnostic categories.

The results were supportive. First, let me say that depressed patients improved with both forms of Attitude Therapy investigated. Patients will therefore respond to Active Friendliness or supportive therapy which historically has been the treatment for depression. However, patients treated on the antidepression program continued to improve or hold their gains through the research period for six months. Subjects on the Active Friendliness program tended to regress. Following treatment on the antidepression program, subjects were less depressed, less dependent upon physical complaints and symptoms, and less self-deceiving. In addition, they were less confused, anxious, ruminative, and repressed. They had a more positive self-concept and manifested improved interpersonal relationships with family members and others. The group treated on the antidepression program without medication or placebo made greater gains than any other group. The mean test profile was significantly more normal in appearance at the last evaluation. The addition of placebos or antidepressant medications as prescribed in this study did not improve the effectiveness of the two forms of Attitude Therapy in relieving depression.

The antidepression program utilizing the Attitude of Kind Firmness is a safe and effective treatment technique.

A number of other comparisons support the above conclusions. Patients on the antidepression program spent an average of 14 days less time in the hospital during this study than did the patients on the Active Friendliness program. One patient on Active Friendliness remained depressed throughout the six months of the study but quickly responded to treatment on the antidepression program. Five patients assigned to Active Friendliness had to be removed because of a dangerous increase of psychological disturbance. These patients improved when treated with Kind Firmness. No patients required removal from the antidepression program because of increased disturbance. Many patients on the antidepression program spontaneously commented to the effect that the problems they had prior to hospitalization still existed, but that they had changed so that they were now able to face and deal with them.

Following is a case history of the use of the Active Friendliness Attitude:

A young sailor came to us following several months of hospitalization in the Navy. As a part of his illness, he believed that electricity jumped into his body when he touched a large coffee urn. He believed the electricity affected his entire body—particularly his sexual organs, leaving him impotent. Immediately after receiving the imaginary shock, the patient hid under a table. When he was found sometime later, he was uncommunicative. He remained this way through several months of active treatment on psychiatric wards in the Navy. He was transferred to a V.A. Hospital, awaiting discharge from the Navy.

On the day after his admission to the hospital, a student nurse and a nursing assistant took the patient for a walk on the hospital grounds. The patient seemed to enjoy the outing, but he remained essentially noncommunicative.

From the time of the invasion of his body by the electricity, the patient had been incontinent of urine. He was unkept in his personal appearance. He showed little interest in anything. On the third day of hospitalization, his case was presented to the Treatment Planning Conference. After his case history had been reviewed, the patient was brought into the conference room by a nursing assistant. He had to be led into the room. He sat slumped over, his arms limply by his side, refusing to look at anyone. He was told by the interviewer that we were glad he had come to our hospital and that we would help him avoid failure in the future.

We told him we believed he was afraid and that we understood his fear and respected it. We told him we were going to be his friends and that there was nothing he could ask that we would not attempt to grant.

The patient sat very still during this conversation. He said nothing. He was then told that he could go back to the ward. He made no move to leave. Since he was on Active Friendliness, we could not, of course, force him to go. Finally, he was asked if he wanted to say something to the group. He sat up in the chair, raised his head, looked out at the group and said, "I feel like I am coming out of a long dream."

The Treatment Team members were shocked. The patient's voice had an eerie, dreamlike quality about it. It was a most impressive experience. The patient was told to go back to the ward with the nursing assistant. He did so willingly. We thought that he had, in a short time, become a different person.

From the time of the dramatic moment in the Treatment Planning Conference, the patient took an active interest in his own grooming. He ceased being incontinent of urine. He shaved himself. On the day after the staff conference, he asked for ground privileges. These were granted. He started showing an active interest in everything going on around him, he talked quite freely with other patients as well as with staff members, and he became involved in a game of checkers with the ward nurse. The patient, for the first time, showed interest in hearing from his family. His parents were contacted and they came to visit. He began making plans for the future.

In many mental hospitals the nurse supervisor of a large unit would not become involved in treatment. However, in our hospital everyone tries to use all of their skills. The supervisory nurse would take this patient with her on routine rounds and, on several occasions, took him over to the main building when she went to sign time cards. Occasionally, she took him for brief visits with the chief nurse. Since the chief nurse knew of the prescription of Active Friendliness, she also participated actively in the treatment of the patient.

Within five days after the Treatment Planning Conference, this patient had been transferred to a fully open ward where he had full self-care responsibility. Six weeks later he went on a visit with his family and plans were made for his discharge from the hospital.

## No Demand

By No Demand Attitude we mean that we place no demands whatsoever on the patient. This attitude is used when the patient is trying to destroy everything around him. We believe that the individual is in a state of fear which he tries to overcome by frightening the world away through threatening the world with destruction. He feels pressured by the demands of society. Our treatment efforts are to remove the feeling of pressure which is overwhelming the patient. We tell the patient that we have three rules: (1) He may not leave our treatment program without our permission; (2) he may not hurt himself; and, (3) he may not hurt anyone else. With the exception of these three rules, the patient may do anything. We have observed that no matter how destructive the patient is, if he does not get positive feedback of counter-aggression, he will rapidly settle down. (One can't fight too well if he has no one to fight with.) We rarely see rage episodes lasting longer than a few minutes. It seems much longer but when the staff can stand calmly by and see that the three rules are maintained, we see the behavior quickly modified and the patient able to become calm.

## Passive Friendliness

The Passive Friendliness Attitude is similar to Active Friendliness Attitude with one very important difference—we wait for the patient to make the first move. Essentially, the treatment team is saying to the patient, "We are here to help you. We know you are frightened of other people. You are suspicious. You find it difficult to relate yourself to other people. Therefore, we will not move in too close. We will be available to help you if you wish to call on us. You may ask us for anything you want. We will try to meet your requests. We will not push in too close to you because we believe this would frighten you." This Attitude of Passive Friendliness is prescribed for the suspicious, paranoid individual.

## Matter-of-Fact

The last attitude is Matter-Of-Factness. This is the way we deal with everybody in our day-to-day relationships.

My wife, a mid-Westerner and a former music therapist at the Menninger Clinic, has used Attitude Therapy for years. She says I should not tell southerners that Matter-Of-Fact Attitude is the same as the way in which we deal with each other on a day-to-day basis. Southerners are rarely very matter-of-fact in their day-to-day relationships. They most frequently cover everything up with a lot of sweetness and light. So she said tell Attitude Therapy Trainees that it is like a Yankee's normal day-to-day relationship. It is the way you deal matter-of-factly without adding honey and sugar and magnolia blossoms to your communications. What we are trying to do with this

Attitude is to make the patient aware of the fact that we have no magic. We do not believe medicines will cure him. We tell then, "There's no magic. It's up to you. You're going to have to prove to yourself and to society that you can meet the demands placed on you." We are treating psychopaths and alcoholics with this approach. So far we are very pleased with some of the things that are happening in these very difficult groups of patients. The value of "talking therapy" surely must have been demonstrated to you at this Institute. I am dedicated to the idea that interpersonal relations are the most important factor in the treatment of the mentally ill. I believe, further, that interpersonal encounters can be prescribed and carried out by both professional and paraprofessional staffs, not only in mental hospitals but in penal institutions, schools, and even in family living. In other words, I believe human behavior can be understood and changes can be predicted and brought about. I hope I have made it abundantly clear that I am not a believer in the magic of medicines, but a firm believer in interpersonal relationships.

## Chapter 10

# CHEMOTHERAPY AND THE BEHAVIORAL DISORDER

Leonard Horecker

The treatment modalities available in our institutions are numerous. In this paper, Doctor Horecker describes one approach to dealing with the patient whose pathology includes the problem of acting out violently toward his environment. Specifically, he utilizes an intensive medication program to control the patient's overt behavior. Doctor Horecker believes that employing such a procedure allows the patient to be accessible more quickly to psychotherapy, which he regards to be the basic therapy. It is his experience that medication can be used safely and in large doses in order to expedite the patient's ability to participate in this process. He describes several cases in which such an approach was successfully employed.

Editors

The classical dictum regarding drugs when I was in medical school was, "Use the least amount to achieve the greatest therapeutic effectiveness, considering at all times the safety of the patient." Regretably, total ideas are often handled in a fragmented and compartmentalized fashion. This applies to the idea regarding amount and effectiveness of drugs. Although, therapeutic effectiveness must be and obviously is the goal of the physician, this goal seems to be relegated to a preconscious position. Presumably, it operates all the time, sort of unconsciously, like a so-called habit. What appears to remain on the surface, all too often, is the idea of "least amount" as an abstraction and unrelated to the needs or safety of the patient. The reasons for what amounts often to an overcautiousness are perhaps not relevant at this moment.

In psychiatry generally, and in mental hospitals particularly, often inadequate amounts of medication are used. This leads to unfortunate situations. The patient does not improve, in fact the patient's condition may worsen. At times this is blamed upon the drug as being ineffective, and another drug is started with the same unhappy results. Many times the patient, having an "awareness" of his illness, becomes discouraged and additionally distrustful. The personnel working with the patient, including the physician, also become discouraged and may lose sight of the patient in the "busyness" of everyday work. Worse still, the personnel may become afraid of the patient. Then mismanagement of various sorts follows.

In the mental hospitals are people with serious disorders of thought, affect, and character. Frequently, the nature of the illness, regardless of which of the three areas is principally involved, produces external behavior, which is an acting out of the internal disturbance that is not acceptable to the hospital milieu. The range of behavioral activities, whether it is in the form of some sort of self-abuse or is belligerence, aggressiveness, or combativeness toward the environment, must be dealt with effectively and rapidly for the safety of the patient and the immediate environment. When the patient's behavior becomes realistically or unrealistically intolerable to the personnel, and all so-called appropriate measures have failed, then the patient is regarded as a foreign object that must be gotten rid of as soon as possible. Needless to say, this is often necessary and appropriate. It is at this point, in Illinois, that a male patient is transferred to Illinois Security Hospital.

Prior to the advent of the tranquilizers as we know them today, sedatives, hydrotherapy, restraints, Metrazol®, insulin, and electric therapy were utilized with varying degrees of effectiveness in endeavoring to deal with the mental and external behavioral aberrations of the mentally ill person. As has been well-documented, the tranquilizers, and later the antidepressants, introduced a new era in the treatment of emotional disorders generally and allowed for a new atmosphere to emerge and exist within the mental hospital.

At Illinois Security Hospital, there are, from a legal viewpoint, essentially four categories of patients: (1) The patient who has allegedly committed a crime and has been found incompetent to stand trial; (2) The patient presenting a behavioral problem at another state facility; (3) A small group of adolescents transferred for treatment from a Department of Corrections juvenile facility; and,

(4) A small group transferred or committed for treatment from the penitentiary.

Presently, there are approximately 280 patients at Illinois Security Hospital. This is a relatively small but highly specific group of people. They have in common, in addition to being mentally ill, that they acted out aggressively, often violently toward their community, whether it was "in the street" or in a hospital. This compact group of irritable, aggressive, confused, often frightened, delusional, and hallucinating people, in close contact with each other and staff, creates an atmosphere that is potentially explosive.

With the use of the tranquilizers, the high degree of tension and the explosiveness have been reduced markedly in most, if not all, situations. What has emerged is an atmosphere in which therapeutic programs can function and flourish. Patients, who formerly had to be constantly kept in isolation because they attacked someone, are now able to be on the open unit and participate in planned activities immediately upon their release from isolation. Patients, even those in isolation, who abused themselves by various sorts of mutilation including striking their heads violently against the walls, now no longer engage in this kind of behavior. Patients, who cowered in isolated areas for fear of attack and often lashed out suddenly against another patient or staff member who they phantasized was about to attack them, now are less fearful, less delusional, less a threat, and are able to interact acceptably in group situations. Adolescents, who engaged in constant "horse play" leading to serious fights and injuries, or who acted-out in constant rebellion as they did on the streets, have been integrated acceptably into the social milieu of the hospital.

These alterations in behavior were accomplished by using the tranquilizers widely, and often dramatically, as a base upon which other therapeutic procedures could then be used effectively. The tranquilizers utilized are generally considered the major tranquilizers. The minor or medium strength tranquilizers have extremely limited value in the setting described.

Chlorpromazine, perphenazine, and recently, chlorprothixene and thiothixene are the principle drugs used at Illinois Security Hospital. Thioridazine, although reported to be as effective as chlorpromazine, has not controlled agitation or anxiety nearly as well with this group of patients. Beyond 600 to 800 mg per day, thioridazine has not seemed to show any additional therapeutic effectiveness. Trifluoperazine, a potent tranquilizer and presumably equal to perphenazine in strength, has not seemed to demonstrate the same antipsychotic capability as has perphenazine.

Every new patient is seen for an initial psychiatric examination shortly after admission. Immediately following admission, if the patient shows agitation, anxiety, insomnia, refuses food, or is expressing frank psychotic material, the standing orders go into effect. Chlorpromazine 200 mg q.i.d. and perphenazine 8 mg q.i.d. are prescribed. Trihexyphenidyl HCl 2 mg and Phenobarbital ¼ or ½ grain are prescribed with each dose of the tranquilizer prophylactically. This is to prevent not only Parkinsonian symptoms but also the increase in muscle tension caused by the alerting tranquilizers such as perphenazine and thiothixene. If the patient will not accept this medication orally, intramuscular injection of both perphenazine and chlorpromazine is ordered. Chlorpromazine can be given intramuscularly in very limited amounts because of the small concentration of the drug per cc and because giving more than 2 cc's per injection site often produces pain, induration, and sloughing of tissue. Injections are made in both hips if necessary. However, if the patient's agitation and/or combativeness does not become ameliorated within several hours or less, sleep is induced with sodium amobarbital. Initially, sodium amobarbital is used intravenously. Up to 15 grains are given very slowly. Resuscitation and oxygen equipment are in ready use. Once sleep is induced, it is maintained with intramuscular injection of 3¾ to 7½ grains every three to six hours depending upon circumstances. The rationale for induction of sleep is to interfere with the internal mechanism producing the condition, to reach toward a more homeostatic level within the patient. Often upon awakening or a day or two later, the patient has much less tension and more routine procedures can be applied.

A word about approaching a patient threatening to fight or already fighting—the approach has to be organized and planned. At least four staff are necessary to carry out the plan successfully. Each staff member is assigned an extremity. The objective is to move in and take hold of the assigned extremity, not to push, punch, twist, or whatever. Simply take hold of and hold the extremity. If each of the four carries out the instructions, the patient usually can be subdued with minimal to no harm.

During the initial examination, an assessment is made of the patient's mental condition. The usual areas, such as sensorium, affect, nature of speech, thought processes, judgment, and insight, if any, are noted. If possible, the discussion involves the reason the patient was admitted to Illinois Security Hospital, at least as he sees it. The patient's story is often, if not usually, in considerable variance with the reports of behavior that accompany the patient to the hospital. The material elicited at this time is used later as a base line to measure degrees of improvement or regression that may occur.

If the patient shows an overt psychotic condition and/or there is a history of marked acting-out at the previous facility, then the medication is started as follows: Chlorpromazine 200 to 300 mg q.i.d. depending upon the degree of disorganization of the patient and/or history of acting-out; perphenazine 8 mg q.i.d., and to be increased to 16 mg q.i.d. in two days; trihexyphenidyl and phenobarbital as previously indicated. Liquid phenobarbital is used particularly because patients have been known to save the tablets and use them in a large single dose in suicidal attempts.

If the patient is a chronic schizophrenic with a long history of hospitalization, he probably will not be seen by me again for a month unless called to my attention sooner by nursing staff, aides, or mental health workers. The less disturbed and the acute disorders are seen again within a week or two, sometimes twice in the same week to observe directly the patient's reaction to the medication.

It has been noted that patients in an acute confusional state respond positively, more quickly, and to lower doses. Extra-pyramidal side effects are not seen primarily in this group, but rather a general retardation of motion and speech. The angry, agitated, rebellious, and those with great anxiety and paranoid-like thought processes seem to be able to tolerate a far greater amount of phenothiazines without showing any significant side effects.

If the patient's total behavior has not altered when next seen, the combination of tranquilizers are increased. Chlorpromazine will be increased from 200 to 400 or 500, or from 300 to 500 or 600 mg q.i.d., depending upon reported and observed behavior. Perphenazine is increased to 20 mg q.i.d.

By the time the level of medication has reached 500 to 600 mg of chlorpromazine and 20 mg of perphenazine per dose respectively, the patient's external behavior has come under control and he can now be fully incorporated into the total program of the hospital.

It should be stated that most often the increase in medication occurs over a period of two to four weeks. At times, however, it is necessary to use the drugs more dramatically. There are occasions when the initial dose of chlorpromazine is 500 mg and may be altered to 700 or 800 mg per dose, always or most always on a q.i.d. basis, within 48 hours. This occurs when the patient is particularly highly agitated, reacting to and trying to act-out his delusional system, and shows no indication of a decrease in this behavior in the first two days.

While the patient remains actively psychotic, the medication continues to be increased but at a slower rate. More time is allowed for the medication to have an effect, if it is going to, upon the psychophysiological system. In selected cases, the chlorpromazine may need to be increased gradually at intervals of one to two months to a level of 1000 to 1200 mg per dose. The level has, on rare occasions, been raised to 1300 and 1400 mg per dose. At this point, the delusional system became less active and the patient began to show signs of endeavoring to reorganize his thought processes along more realistic lines. If the hallucinatory process is still operating as it sometimes has, perphenazine is increased to 24 and 28 mg q.i.d. Frequently, at these levels, the hallucinations cease. If the patient maintains the improved state, reductions occur approximately every four to six weeks.

When positive changes do not occur, thiothixene is substituted for perphenazine beginning at 30 mg per dose. Although thiothixene has been used for a relatively short period of time, it has recently been observed that at 50 mg per dose, the delusional system begins to fragment and the patient begins to "look" at his thoughts more objectively.

We ran electrocardiograms on a small group of about ten patients receiving over 1000 mg of chlorpromazine per dose. In about $\frac{1}{2}$ to $\frac{3}{4}$, changes, particularly in the T-wave were noted. The T-wave was either of low intensity, isotonic, or inverted. The chlorpromazine was reduced to 800 or 900 mg in these patients. Two or three months later, the ECG's were repeated. In some, the T-waves seemed to be returning to a more normal state. The number of cases observed is too small to be significant, but may warrant further study.

When the patients are able, increasingly, to deal effectively in their relationships with others, medication is gradually reduced. Even though medication effectively controls external behavior, as it frequently does, illogical thought processes often remain intact. Nevertheless, this does not necessarily interfere with a patient's ability to make an acceptable or uneventful adjustment to his environment. At such times, the chlorpromazine is gradually reduced and the perphenazine or thiothixene is maintained at 20 mg or higher. If this level had not been attained previously, the alerting tranquilizer is increased at this point. The purpose of the medication, as already stated, is to gain control over aberrant external and internal behavior, and to provide a base upon which other therapeutic procedures may be successfully applied. Some of the patients, particularly the ones with characterological disorders, have viewed the medication, generally, and chlorpromazine and chlorprothixene specifically, as punishment. Even though they have been advised repeatedly that chlorpromazine is used to help them exercise control over their impulses and punishment is not intended, they maintain their views. This may have proven beneficial in the long run. As they have continued to act out, the level was increased. Most have "given up" by the time 800 to 1000 mg per dose was reached. In one instance, a young patient, who may have entered into brief periods of psychosis, indicated, "I am an animal from the jungle—you treat me like an animal—I'll be an animal." His aggressive destructive behavior slowed down but still continued past 1000 mg per dose. At 1500 mg q.i.d., he finally gave up his battle. From that point on, increasingly, his behavior improved, and it could be said that he became a model patient considering his former activities. Thus, it can be noted that in specific instances and with certain patients, the medication exerts a control that is in addition to the one intended. This control is ultimately significant in helping to bring about acceptable ideas and behavior in the patient.

Illinois Security Hospital provides a structured environment not found at other state hospitals. Frequently, disorganized and regressed patients are unable to handle the responsibility given to them at the regular state hospitals. At Illinois Security Hospital, the patient's responsibility for dealing with choices is more limited. When a patient's external behavior has been brought under control, the question of a transfer to a hospital of lesser security is raised. In my estimation, a patient is ready for a transfer only when there has been a significant improvement in his thought processes. If transferred prior to such a time, it can reasonably be expected that he will act out again and most likely in the same way that originally brought him to Illinois Security Hospital. The fact that he is adjusting successfully in a highly structured environment is, in itself, not a sufficient basis for consideration of transfer.

Among the problems of patients who are adjudicated incompetent to stand trial is the use of drugs. By and large, it seems that the courts will not permit a patient a competency hearing if drugs, even in small maintenances doses, are being used. Perhaps it is the "court psychiatrist" who is the real obstacle. It appears reasonable that if a person can function rationally and relevantly, free of illogical and inconsistent thought processes by using small amounts of a tranquilizer, he ought to be allowed a hearing and be considered competent. This is what individuals using insulin or thyroid medication are currently permitted, all else being equal. This is an area in which the law and psychiatry need to establish a new understanding.

The point that is being made, basically, is that the major tranquilizers referred to can be used in large doses and combinations with safety. No significant side effects have occurred. Routine examination, at regular intervals, of the blood count and urinalysis have not recorded any pathology. This is not a plea to use large doses for the sake of large doses. Instead, what is being said is that, at all times, the dosage and combination of drugs ought to be sufficient to control the symptoms. While this control is in effect, the greatest safety will be provided for the patient and the community in which he resides.

In conclusion, I want to state that although I have been talking of chemotherapy and certainly use drugs extensively, I consider psychotherapy the basic therapy. In the cases we are working with at Illinois Security Hospital, drugs provide a vehicle upon which psychotherapy can be utilized effectively in eliminating the basic internal nuclei that produce the symptoms. It is toward this ultimate end that we ought to strive.

## Chapter 11

# REALITY THERAPY AND CAMPUS PRISONS

Leonard Zunin

Reality Therapy has attracted a considerable number of proponents. Doctor Zunin is a particularly articulate spokesman for this therapeutic approach. His paper presents an unusually clear introduction to the assumptions and philosophy from which the principles of Reality Therapy emerged. These principles are then enumerated and illustrated in the context of the therapeutic relationship.

The second section of Doctor Zunin's paper should be of particular relevance to those interested in innovative programming in the field of corrections. Specifically, he presents the concept of constructing prisons in the United States on university campuses. He challenges our correctional system to take this step. Doctor Zunin believes that such a move would have a major impact in the success of our rehabilitation efforts.

EDITORS

W E ARE BEGINNING TO SEE that in the field of corrections there are many approaches to the same problem, but clearly there is a problem. We are living in a world of dynamic change. Dr. Albert J. Glass and Professor Merle Alexander in their lectures also emphasized how much is changing, how rapidly the changes are occurring, and what a dynamic state of change the entire field of corrections is in, and has been undergoing, during the last few decades.

To me, there is a parallel in what has been happening in child care, and I see child care as akin to social change. Since the dawn of history, people have had trouble raising children. Adam and Eve had a lot of trouble. They had the first problem kids, Cain and Abel, and they just did not know how to handle them. Parents from that time on have been seeking alternatives and approaches to handling their problem children. At the turn of the century, before people like Dobson, Ginott, Spock and Gesell, the mothers of this country did not know where to turn. So, they turned to the government.

They turned to the Department of Labor and the Children's Bureau because they published a pamphlet on how to raise children. If you look at those pamphlets through the years, you will see that the first pamphlets they published around 1912 or 1913 dealt with child rearing in very definitive and exact terms. And if you look at the pamphlets of today, they are full of qualifying ifs, ands, buts, and sometimes, which were not present in the first pamphlets.

For example, in 1929 the pamphlets taught the mothers that thumbsucking was considered extremely dangerous and suggested tying the child's hands behind his back. That was in 1929. In 1962 they changed their tune and said, perhaps the child has a problem. Try to learn what it is. The last pamphlet said, maybe it is not the child who has a problem. Perhaps, it is you, mother. Perhaps, you have a problem in understanding that the child receives some pleasure, some oral gratification from thumbsucking.

With regard to toilet training, the early books said, the child must begin toilet training before one year of age. Do not let is go too long. In 1945, they had new scientific evidence. They said, don't rush! Take it easy, because an attempt to toilet train made too soon is useless and frustrating. And in 1955 they implored mothers to please, whatever you do, go slowly. Do not rush the child.

In 1929 if a child played with his genitals, it was described as a fierce impulse to be controlled. In 1942 they said, it is just idle exploration, but it is not good. Try to find a toy and put it in the child's hand. In 1962 they said, do not worry about it. It's alright. And whatever you do, don't give the child the idea that the genital area is evil, bad, or dirty.

In 1942 it was suggested that it was alright to cuddle the child only on schedule, at a certain time during the day. In 1955 they said do it whenever you want, and the more you do it the better.

To me, there is a great parallel between child rearing and corrections. It is time we considered changes in our traditional methods in corrections, and that is what this Institute is all about. We are taking another long, hard look at our traditional approaches and the traditional approaches and the traditional modes with which we go about trying to solve these problems related to corrections.

The following are some statistics that put the problem in bold relief. We have a murder every 36 minutes in this country; a forceable rape every 15 minutes; an aggravated assault every two minutes; a robbery every two minutes; every minute, nine serious crimes. Every 36 seconds in the United States, there is an auto theft; every 21 seconds, a larceny; and, every 16 seconds, a burglary. In 1969, serious crimes were up 11 percent over the 1968 rate. In 1963, there were 55 policemen murdered, in 1969, 73. In 1963, there were 16,793 assaults on police officers. In 1968, there were 33,604 assaults on police officers.

Whatever we are doing, our deterrent to crime, our attempts at rehabilitation, just are not effective enough. We have now probably well over 100,000 laws to enforce the Ten Commandments, increasing them at a very rapid rate. I am aware that federal programs and state programs that effect changes in the legal system take time and patience.

Reality Therapy is one approach to correcting behavior. There are many approaches, and this is one which we find effective for helping people move from what we refer to as a failure identity to a success identity. It was first developed by Dr. William Glasser in a California Youth Authority facility, Ventura School for Girls.

In Reality Therapy, we believe that whatever we are in the present represents the sum total of everything that has gone on before, that our current behavior is a reflection of our past history, and that we are continually changing. We also believe that it is important to determine what we are trying to correct before we correct it. Perhaps, some of the problems presented in this volume raise just that question: What is the problem we are trying to correct? What is a problem for one person may not be a problem for another.

We believe that the mentally ill and the mentally disordered offender are a rarity as, I think, is emphasized in the paper by Dr. Russell O. Settle, Sr. I believe it is an extreme rarity—the truly mentally disordered offender. The mentally ill and the offender are generally suffering from the same malady. They are unwilling to take full responsibility for their own behavior. Whether we are dealing with the offender or someone who is having other serious problems, no change can occur until an individual begins to believe that he is responsible for his own behavior. Until that is acknowledged, you are not going to make a dent in the sociological system or on an individual basis.

A few years ago, the federal government was interested in determining whether or not the usual criteria which we use to predict success or failure for children in school were valid criteria, such as I.Q.—a traditional estimate to determine whether or not someone has a good chance of succeeding. We were beginning to question these previously held criteria and with increasing doubt.

In the Coleman Report that came out in 1966 were some astounding findings. To me, they were astounding and dramatic. For example, they found that in schools using Title I funds, the best determinant of whether or not a child was going to make it, whether or not a child was going to succeed, was the degree to which that child felt, "I'm responsible for my behavior. I may not make it or I may. If I do, it is because of the things that I do. If I don't make it, it is because of the things that I do." If the child feels "I am the captain of my soul, the master of my fate," he has that sense of individual responsibility. Regardless of all the other factors, his chances of making it in the world are greater. The more a child said, "If I went to another school where my friends go, if I had better books, if my sister would just shut up when I study at night, if I had sharper pencils, if I had a different place to study," the more he saw what happened to him as being secondary from the outside, the greater were the chances that kid was not going to make it regardless of his I.Q. That same principle, at least in my experience, applies to individual therapy, to family therapy, to multiple family therapy, and to others. The family that feels "we are responsible for what happens to us" has a greater chance of succeeding.

The whole notion of causation is exceedingly important and it is one of the tremendous advances made in the helping professions. But some people believe that if we are trying to produce change, it is our job in working with people to work with "whys" or causes for their behavior. It is *not* our job to provide explanations for irresponsible behavior, but rather to help people become more responsible. It is a subtle shift, but it has important ramifications.

We, in Reality Therapy, also make the assumption that for the most part people know the difference between right and wrong. In the military I talked with many people in the brig, many people who were apprehended on offenses. I have talked with hundreds of girls at the Ventura School for Girls. Each time I saw a girl I asked, "At the time you did what you did, did you know it was wrong?" I never heard a girl say, "No, I didn't know." They always said, "Yes, I knew, but I didn't care," or "I wanted to do it anyway," or "What did I have to lose," "What the hell," and so on, "But I knew there was a rule against it, that it was wrong." In trying to work with people, some therapists spend many hours dealing with such questions as, "Are you sure you knew it was wrong, was it wrong, or wasn't it wrong?" That really does not help. It wastes precious time.

We in Reality Therapy also make another assumption and that is, in general, it is a good idea for the therapist to be healthier than the patient, at least in the areas in which we are trying to help them. If someone has had some problems and has successfully solved them, he may function even better. That is the basis for Synanon, Alcoholics Anonymous, Neurotics Anonymous, and others. These people who have solved the problems and gained some tools of understanding and insight can help others wrestling with similar problems. However, if an alcoholic is trying to help another alcoholic and is taking a "nip" while he is talking with him, he won't be much help.

We also believe that involvement, the *need* for involvement, is hereditary. If you do not have water to drink, you get thirsty. Thirst in its extreme form is painful. If you do not have food, you get hungry; hunger can be very, very painful. If you don't get involved, you get very lonely. Loneliness is the greatest of all human pain. When a person is placed in a sensory-isolation experiment for hours, suspended in water with their eyes covered, their ears blocked and so on, trying to block off all their senses, what happens? Normal individuals begin to hallucinate. What do they hallucinate? They hallucinate other people. Solitary confinement is, by all standards and by all cultures the worst, most inhumane, cruel, and painful of all human punishments.

No one ever chooses to be lonely. This has nothing to do with choosing to be alone. We all chose to be alone on an intermittent basis frequently in our lives, but no one wants to be lonely. We all *need* to be involved with other people whether we have a success or a failure identity. The basic principles of Reality Therapy are guidelines for becoming involved with people and helping them to change.

Reality Therapy was developed by Dr. William Glasser, a psychiatrist in Southern California, in the late 1950's. It is a series of theoretical concepts and principles applicable not only to individuals with behavioral and emotional problems but also valuable as an approach for any individual or group seeking either to gain a success identity for themselves and/or to help others toward this same goal.

The first important step in changing behavior is to find out what the behavior is we are trying to correct. No matter how cruel and unusual are the circumstances which led to a person's behavior, we must make it clear to him that past events are not to be used as an excuse for behaving in an irresponsible manner. No matter what "happened" to him in the past, he still must take the full responsibility for what he does *now*.

Until an individual can accept the fact that he is responsible for what he does, there can be no treatment. It is not up to us, as therapists, to advance explanations for irresponsibility. We recognize that individual responsibility is the goal of treatment and unhappiness is the result and not the cause of irresponsibility.

Reality Therapy is based upon the premise that there is a single basic need that all people in all cultures possess from birth to death, that is the need for an identity: to feel that we are somehow separate and distinct from every other living being and that no matter where we go we will not find another person who thinks, looks, acts, and talks exactly like us. This need is universal and transcends all cultures. Its significance is evidenced, for example, in religious teachings of both primitive and civilized societies.

Further, it is not sufficient to realize that one is a distinct entity, but in addition one must have meaning associated with his identity, which is primarily based upon his involvement with others.

Reality Therapy differs from other therapeutic endeavors, such as psychoanalysis, the strict behavioral therapies like operant conditioning, and from some of the newer therapeutic fads in that it is applied not only to the problems of people who are extremely irresponsible and incompetent, but also to the modes of daily living.

Once the ability for successful involvement has been established, the principles of Reality Therapy then evolve into a system or a way of life which helps a person to become successful in almost all of his endeavors. If he is not successful, we try at least to understand where he lacks success and try, even if success seems impossible, in one direction after another to understand that the options are never really closed. There are innumerable options in society to find success one way or another.

Each individual feels that he is relatively successful or unsuccessful. We are not referring to success as measured in titles, or labels, or finances, but rather success in terms of the individual's own self-image, which may or may not conform to the image that others have of him. It is indeed possible for an individual to regard himself as basically a failure in life when others around him regard him as an important success.

Formation of a success or failure identity seems to begin at age four or five, coincidental with the age at which the child enters school. It is at about this age that we find the individual developing the social skills, verbal skills, intellect and thinking ability which enable him to begin to define himself in terms of being a successful or unsuccessful person. In later years, the individual who regards himself as successful appears to associate with other successful people, and vice versa, with increasing divergence.

Individuals who have a success identity have two traits that are consistent and ever-present. First, they know that there is at least one other person who loves them for what they are, and they love at least one other person. Second, individuals with a success identity have the knowledge and understanding most of the time that they are worthwhile human beings and, at least one, and hopefully more than one other individual also feels they are worthwhile. We view worth and love as two very different elements.

The identity that we develop comes from our involvement with others as well as our involvement with ourselves. Our identity develops from recalling objects of one's love and gratification because that which we love and have loved tends to be associated with and psychologically incorporated into ourselves; and what we admire, we tend to exemplify; what we dislike, we tend to reject. We also discover our identity by observing those causes or concerns with which we are involved.

Others also play an important role in helping us to clarify and understand our identity. What others reflect back to us, if we are willing to give our eyes and ears the freedom to see and hear, is a most meaningful mirror of one's identity. This occurs in psychotherapy and in friendships. Our beliefs and value systems, our religion or lack of religion, and philosophy further clarify our identity. We also see ourselves in relation to the living conditions, the climate, and economic and social status of others.

Our physical image in relation to others, including our physical structure, our grooming, and our clothes, helps us to see ourselves in relation to others and to clarify our own identity.

Those individuals who appear to develop a failure identity and have difficulty and feel a sense of discomfort in the real world handle this sense of discomfort in two general ways. They may either *deny* reality or *ignore* it. What we consider mental illness is the various ways in which an individual denies reality. Mental illness may manifest itself in a wide variety of ways. In Reality Therapy, we do not believe that specific diagnostic terms are helpful or useful in providing an effective method of change for the mentally ill. The person who is mentally ill has changed the real world in his own fantasy to make himself feel more comfortable. He denies reality to protect himself from facing the feeling or being meaningless and insignificant in the world around him. For example, both the grandiose delusion and the persecutory delusion of the so-called schizophrenic provide the same support. Is there any difference between the individual who believes that the FBI, the CIA, the President, and all of the political leaders are following him, and the person who believes he is Jesus, or Napoleon, or God, or the Governor, or the President? Both individuals are changing the world in their own mind and in their own fantasy to assist them in feeling meaningful and significant in the world.

Those individuals who ignore reality are people whom we believe are aware of the real world and choose, rather than to deny and change reality in their own mind, to simply ignore it. These individuals are referred to as delinquents, criminals, sociopaths, personality disorders, etc. They are basically the antisocial individuals who choose to break the rules and regulations of society on a regular basis, thereby ignoring reality.

## THE BASIC PRINCIPLES OF REALITY THERAPY

The Principles of Reality Therapy are outlined in a particular order. This order is meant to be flexible and workable and is not, in any way, a rigid or fixed system. We find, in working with individuals, that this general framework provides helpful guidelines and important and basic principles in utilizing a wide variety of specific techniques. Basic to Reality Therapy, as outlined above, is the concept of involvement. In fact, for purposes of psychotherapy, we believe that involvement and motivation can be considered synonymous. The first three principles are ways in which the therapist becomes responsibly involved with the person he is trying to help.

### Principle I: Personal

Basic to Reality Therapy is that the therapist must communicate that he cares, that he is warm, personal, and friendly. Aloofness and cool detachment are not therapeutic. Warmth, understanding, and realistic concern and interest are the cornerstones of effective treatment.

The use of personal pronouns by both the therapist and the patient such as *I* and *me* and *you,* rather than *it,* or *you all,* or *one does,* or *out there,* or *they,* assist to facilitate involvement.

Being personal also means that the therapist is willing, if indicated and appropriate, to discuss his own experiences. He is willing to have his values challenged and discussed. He is willing to demonstrate that he acts in a responsible manner and is willing to admit that he is far from being perfect or free of concerns. In contrast to attempting to enhance a transference or distorted image of the therapist, the reality therapist presents himself as he is—a real and genuine person, interested in the individual with whom he is working.

Being personal in Reality Therapy also means caring, and caring in a therapeutic sense is following through with a commitment or a promise. It is when we do not care about someone or something that we generally do not follow through with what we say.

Lastly, being personal means conveying to the individual, verbally but usually nonverbally, your sincere belief that they have the ability to be happier and do better than they are currently doing; that they are indeed capable of functioning in a more responsible and, there-

fore, a more effective and self-fulfilling manner. In fact, if the therapist does not believe this about the patient, he is doing the patient a
severe disservice by continuing to engage him in a treatment situation.

If the patient does not feel that he is personally accepted by the
individual who is attempting to help him or teach him, his chances
of receiving help or learning are markedly decreased. The purpose
of the first step in Reality Therapy is to help people become involved
with someone who can help them to understand that there is something more to life than focusing on their misery, or their symptoms,
or their irresponsible behavior; to understand that another human
being cares for them. It is important and considered part of the
caring relationship to define the limitations of the involvement. It is
physically and emotionally not possible for a therapist who is attempting to lead a responsible life of his own to become deeply involved in
friendships with everyone who comes to him for help. He becomes
involved and friendly within the context of the office. The therapist
has to be honest about this. He has to explain this to the patient. He
cannot have or imply hidden promises with which he cannot follow
through. The warmth, the concern, the involvement in the therapeutic
relationship is what is essential, rather than the content of the verbal
exchange. This means that in the early discussions of therapy, anything is really open for discussion; and, if the individual is talking
about subjects other than his own misery or problems, this is not seen
as a resistance but rather as something worthwhile and of interest to
both the therapist and the patient. A pure focus on misery tends to
reverse the value of therapy and increase, rather than decrease, the
person's involvement with his own misery.

## Principle II: Focus On Behavior Rather Than Feelings

No one can gain a success identity in society without being aware
of what his behavior is. When a person denies his behavior, becomes
unaware of his behavior, or begins to believe, as has wrongly been
postulated by many psychotherapeutic movements, that his feelings
are more important than his behavior, he will have difficulty gaining
a success identity. It is our contention that there is a basic social
fallacy based upon the notion "When I feel better, I will do more."
We know that this is a cyclical phenomenon, in that when people

feel better, indeed they do more constructive things and when they do more, they feel better. When we complete work we have been procrastinating or avoiding, we do feel better; but, also, when we feel better we do more work. The fallacy lies in the notion that it is easier to make ourselves feel better than to stimulate ourselves to action and thereby feel better. Feeling and doing are intimately related, and it is our continuing experience that it is far easier to enter this cycle at the "doing" rather than the "feeling" point.

Further, Reality Therapy rests on the premise that human beings are organisms who think, feel, act, and who have evolved in such a way as to have very limited and very poor control over feeling and thinking. This is exemplified by simple experiments such as trying not to think of the color red for three minutes, or our inability to feel good whenever we wish. If this were possible, we could conveniently pass a law requiring all individuals to feel good at all times. Obviously, this is not the case, and although it is often not recognized by individuals in the field of mental health, it has been recognized for thousands of years by those in the legislative field. There is not a single law on the books that governs thinking or feeling. Reality Therapy is based upon the premise that, since individuals can more easily control their behavior than they can control thinking and feeling, it is indeed on behavior that we must concentrate.

Although it is not usually possible for a person to change his feelings significantly, and over a prolonged period, without first making some kind of change in his behavior. We are not suggesting that feelings are unimportant—they are of utmost importance. If people behave toward each other in a competent, responsible way, then eventually, if not immediately, there are good feelings tied to this relationship.

For example, if an individual comes to the office and states, "I feel miserable and depressed," rather than one of the traditional answers such as silence, or "Tell me more about it," or "Have you had any suicidal thoughts," or "Depressed," or "How long have you felt this way," or "Have you ever felt this depressed at any other time in your life," or others, the reality therapist might respond by saying, "What are you doing to make yourself depressed?" This statement of course does not deny their feelings or say that their feelings are wrong, or insincere, or unimportant but rather, that the therapist is relating these feelings to their behavior. We accept the fact that they are feeling badly and, in fact, that is probably why they came to the therapist. But, when asked what they are doing to make themselves depressed, patients usually respond with amazement. When they begin to outline what they are doing and what they have done over the last few days, it often becomes apparent that any normal, average human being would also be depressed if they were doing the same things. We find that patients begin to regard themselves and their symptoms in a very different light when confronted with the normalcy of their depressive feelings. Patients take a totally different view of themselves and their symptoms when told—if it is applicable—that the therapist would be much more concerned about them if they were doing what they are doing and did not experience a feeling of depression and/or loneliness. This clearly pinpoints the behavior and not the feelings as the problem. The next step in this particular example might be that the therapist would then ask the patient why he is not more depressed. This is a particularly difficult question and a provocative one for most individuals seeking help. When they begin, with the help of the therapist, to outline the various things they are doing with their lives that support them emotionally and assist them from becoming even further depressed, we then are beginning to understand their islands of strength and assist them in becoming aware of their own inner strengths, potentials, and attributes.

We accept the fact that they are feeling badly and that is probably why they came to see a therapist, but individuals are almost invariably surprised when they are asked, "What are you doing?" What our patients are usually telling us is that what they are doing at this time in their lives is not making them feel good and, in fact, is usually making them feel badly. Patients never say to us as therapists, "Tell me what to feel." They only say, "Tell me what to do."

So that, in Reality Therapy, this second main principle is to get the patient's behavior "out on the table" so that they can become aware of it, examine it, and verbally explore it. Unless one becomes aware of his behavior, there is no hope of learning how to behave more competently thereby gaining the success identity, which naturally makes one feel better.

This second principle is probably most poignantly illustrated in the intimate love relationships. The feeling is not self-sustaining without accompanying behavior. Unless the individuals behaviorally relate to each other, do things together, have fun and enjoy each other as human beings and, in doing so, share feelings, the feelings of love and warmth and closeness begin to fade. They have to share behaviors, and only by sharing behavior, whether sexually or in constructive and creative discussion, or in enjoyment, can the relationship live and be sustained and grow.

## *Principle III: Focus On The Present*

In Reality Therapy, we deal with what is going on currently in the person's life—on what the individual is doing now, today, yesterday, or perhaps last week, and also on his present attempts to succeed. This is based upon a conviction that whatever we are today is the sum total of everything that has happened in our lives thus far and that, regardless of how good or bad an individual's past history is, the past is fixed and cannot be changed. All that can be changed is the immediate present and the future.

Again, as when we discussed feelings as related to behavior (it is not that we never talk about feelings but, when we do discuss them we always relate feelings to behavior), we do the same thing with the past and the present. Although the prime focus of discussions in Reality Therapy is on the present and on present attempts to succeed, when the past is discussed incidents are never left as entities in and of themselves but are always related to current behavior. For example, if a person described a crisis experience that occurred several years ago, the therapist will always ask him what he learned from it, how it changed his behavior, and how that change is related to his present behavior and his present attempts to succeed in life.

Further, it appears to us that traditional psychotherapeutic approaches, when discussing the past, often emphasize the traumatic encounters, failures, and difficulties that an individual faced. In Reality Therapy although we de-emphasize the past, when we *do* discuss the past we keep the following factors in mind:

1. We believe that it is quite useful to discuss strengthening and character-building experiences that occurred in the individual's past

life and relate them to current behavior and current attempts to succeed.

2. If we discuss past events, we usually attempt to spend some time discussing other constructive alternatives that the individual might have taken at the time.

3. If we discuss difficulties the individual encountered as a result of his behavior, rather than focusing on a specific difficulty or why the individual "got into so much difficulty," we focus on why the person did not get into more difficulty, what about his behavior was constructive in a positive way that assisted him in avoiding more difficulty, regardless of the degree of difficulty he brought upon himself.

In association with this principle of emphasizing the present rather than the past, we believe that case histories in the traditional format, whether they be by probation officers, psychiatrists, psychologists, social workers and others, are notorious and tragic misrepresentations of individual histories. In fact, any typical case history is not a case history at all, rather it is a "bad case history" in the sense that the traditional history which individuals in the field of mental health counseling are trained to dictate encompass the failures, shortcomings, traumas, and problems with which the person has had to cope. The amount of time, in a typical case history, that is spent on a person's successes, on the assessment of a person's hidden strengths, potentials, and attributes, is sadly minimal. In fact, therapists are not even trained to look for hidden strengths, but rather conditioned to look for failures.

## Principle IV:  Value Judgment

In Reality Therapy, we believe that each individual must make a value judgment about his own behavior and what he is doing to contribute to his own failure before he can be assisted in changing and behavior. Once a person's behavior is clarified, then perhaps for the first time in his life he can begin to look at his behavior critically and judge it on the basis of whether or not it is good for him and for those with whom he is meaningfully involved.

It is our premise that part of emotional health is a willingness to work within the framework of society. We are not saying that individuals should accept society, but rather, if they want to change it or establish a new morality they have to first take responsibility for their own behavior. It is the job of the therapist in discussing the pros and cons of behavior to help the individual acquire all of the related data and approach the decision in a rational manner.

If the therapist makes value judgments for the patient, he is not only imposing his own values on him but also, most importantly, relieving him of the responsibility for his own behavior, and assuming that responsibility himself as the therapist.

## *Principle V: Planning*

Much of the meaningful work of therapy is the process by which we help the individual make specific plans to change behavior. Again, this is true not only of the therapist but also of parents working with children, marital relationships, teachers, employers, and others. It is the job of the therapist to help individuals who often do not know how to plan for more responsible and more competent behavior. Reality Therapy stresses that meaningful and constructive planning is a regular, ongoing, ever-present part of every person's life.

Of course, one of the continual problems in therapy, as well as in all aspects of life, is that once a good plan is made we must develop the strength and the responsibility to implement it. A significant portion of the therapeutic involvement encompasses making plans that are reasonable and realistic and within the motivation and abilities of the patient. The reality therapist must always keep in mind that it is far better to err on the side of making plans that are too simple or too easily carried out than plans that are too complex, thus standing a greater risk of ending in failure. Recalling that from the vantage point of Reality Therapy the people we are trying to help already have as part of their own self-concept a failure identity of some magnitude, it follows then that they will gain a success identity only through successes and not through failures.

One very important aspect of planning is the extreme significance of placing the plan in writing, particularly in the form of a contract between patient and therapist. The differential weight that is attached to the written vs. the spoken word was long ago discovered and successfully utilized by the legal profession—it is time therapists took note. Although this is not always indicated, the reality therapists finds this frequently an exceedingly useful tool.

The reality therapist does not see plans as being absolute, in fact, plans are seen as one way of demonstrating multiple alternatives in life. There is usually a whole variety of plans to solve any problem and, if one's plan does not work there is no harm in going back to make another plan and another plan until an option is arrived at that will work in the situation. To be locked in on one's plan is the same as being involved with one's self and locked into one's misery.

### *Principle VI: Commitment*

Commitment is considered one of the keystones of Reality Therapy. It is only from commitments, from making commitments and following through with those commitments, that we gain a sense of self-worth and maturity in this world. After an individual has made a value judgment about a portion of his behavior and has then been assisted in developing a plan to change that behavior in accordance with his value judgment, the next step is to assist the individual, in a warm and involved manner, to make a commitment to carry out the plan. Making a plan is not enough. It only becomes meaningful if, following the plan, the individual makes a decision of his own volition to execute the plan. The commitment may also be in writing, it may be oral, or it may be both oral and written. Organizations, whether business, professional or helping such as A.A. have, by long experience, been aware that oral and written commitments in front of others assume more binding and meaningful proportions.

### *Principle VII: No Excuses*

Therapists would be naive and foolish to assume that all commitments that a patient makes will be achieved, that all plans will be appropriate and tailored for the situation and will be successful. Plans fail, sometimes frequently, sometimes infrequently; but it is the obligation of the reality therapist to make it clear to the patient that no excuses are acceptable. This means that when the patient explains to the therapist that a particular plan failed, it has been our experience that little therapeutic gain has been noted from challenging or exploring with the patient whether or not the plan failed because of an excuse or for a valid reason.

The therapist does not concern himself with why the plan failed but rather that the plan failed and it is now our job to make a new plan or to modify the old one. Far more therapeutic benefit is gained from working with the patient on redeveloping the plan than in discussing the reasons for the plan's failure. We are therapists and not detectives. We are people relating as human beings and not as lie detectors—we believe people know why things go wrong. Very importantly, the therapist should not demean or depreciate the patient for failing; he should not insult the patient or blame him.

### Principle VIII: Eliminate Punishment

As important as not accepting excuses—and a very difficult thing for most people who are still involved with the old survival morality—is to eliminate punishment when a person fails in a commitment. Punishment, from the vantage point of the reality therapist, is inflicting pain or deprivation of some type for failing to keep a commitment or following through with a plan. Punishment also means not discussing future ways in which the individual can alter his behavior so that he can follow through with a new plan or recommit himself to an old one.

Punishment as a way of changing behavior has rarely worked and works most poorly on those individuals with a failure identity. Although the essential goal of punishment is to get people to change their behavior, we find throughout the history of mankind that pure punishment is an ineffectual social tool for behavioral change.

Therefore, it is important that therapists do not punish patients, that we do not punish them with ridicule, with sarcasm, with hostility, with statements such as, "I knew you would do it, see, you've done it again—you've failed again—I expected it was too much for you— you just don't have what it takes." In making such statements, the therapist punishes the patient and confirms his failure identity.

Punishment is quite different from natural consequences of behavior following contractual planning. For example, if a patient makes a commitment to a child that he is going to allow the child certain privileges if the child accepts certain responsibilities and the child fails in the responsibilities, the parent not only is no longer obligated to keep the commitment, but is not helping the child if he continues to allow the privileges. If the parent says, "You can use the family car on Saturday nights providing you wash it once a week," and the child refuses to wash the car, then the parent has every right to refuse the child the use of the car. This is not punishment. The essence of evoking punishment for planned failures is that being punitive not only reinforces failure identity, but also shatters whatever involvement exists in the therapeutic relationship.

In essence, the reality therapist takes into consideration social issues, values, and concerns. He deals with social organizations, philosophy, and morals. To the extent that he is able to eliminate punishment and not accept excuses for failure, to help the patient substantiate constructive and reasonable value judgments and make plans in accordance with those value judgments, and then help him to make a commitment to follow through with the plan, then we are truly assisting individuals gain a success identity.

## CAMPUS PRISONS

One way in which society reinforces failure identity is through our current prison system. It is clear that our prisons are not working, that the rehabilitation programs are not effective and not sufficient, and that if we are going to do something meaningful in the field of corrections a revision in our concept of the prison system is essential. Dr. Norman I. Barr and I propose that the next fifty prisons in the United States be constructed on college campuses, one in each state. This idea was initially presented at the annual meeting of the American Correctional Association on October 12, 1970. Doctor Barr, who is the former Chief of Psychiatric Services for the Federal Bureau of Prisons and currently the Coordinator of Clinical Services at the Institute for Reality Therapy, Los Angeles, initially proposed this idea. We explored the possibilities, weighed the advantages and disadvantages, and investigated the reactions of others to this idea.

The reactions of individuals learning about this proposal of placing prisons on college campuses are exceedingly varied. Fascinating to us is that the arguments against the proposal are almost identical to the arguments that were presented by both the professional and the lay public when the idea was discussed of making mental hospitals a part of medical schools on college campuses. "You're going to put crazy people on college campuses with healthy students?" "They are going to escape, they are going to rape the students." "We're going to have murders." These were some of the reactions. As we know, utilizing mental hospitals as part of medical schools on college campuses has proven to be valuable, meaningful, and constructive.

American universities, as centers of knowledge, have helped solve problems ranging from the development of the atom bomb to landing a man on the moon. The fields of corrections and academia have always maintained a cool relationship with one another, though the states with the largest universities (California, Illinois, Michigan, and Ohio), also have the largest prisons.

It is our opinion that the placement of prisons on college campuses would be meaningful for the following reasons:

1. It would help educate the public to the fact that resolution of correctional problems is in its own best interests and unequivocably demonstrates correction's determination to find meaningful and viable solutions.

2. If a prison were on a college campus, classes could be held in the prison for education of the ministry, the legal profession, the medical profession, sociologists, social workers, parole officers, hospital administrators, and others. Early in training, these divergent professions could have classes together, at a common meeting ground, centered around the prison system. They could begin to meet and work together because the prison really has the potential of being the soil where so many disciplines can come together and share ideas. These professions in the area of criminology, at the present time, rarely understand one another, have difficulty working together, and yet all have direct or indirect contact with the field of corrections. At the present time, a psychiatric resident takes one or two tours through a prison as a part of a total three-year residency program in psychiatry. Then we wonder why psychiatrists shy away from court work and avoid correctional psychiatry.

3. It is our belief that if the divergent professions noted in point 2 have more exposure to the correctional system, recruitment and interest in this area would increase significantly.

4. It is our belief that if a prison were located on a college campus,

students of various professions would be interested in doing research in the area of criminology. There is a paucity of good information about the mentally disordered offender and the criminal in our society. We need more research and greater understanding if we are going to make progress. We believe that there would be many Master's and Ph.D theses centered around the area of the prisoner and the prison if prisons were geographically convenient to the student. The desperate need that we have, before jumping in feet first to change behavior, is to understand criminal behavior, to understand the causes of aberrant and antisocial behavior and its relationship to our social system.

5. It would provide a soil for recruitment of more effective staff. One of the problems that prisons have is trying to recruit competent staff. Individuals who would be interested and have backgrounds to be effective in the prison system are often not interested in living in a small community out in the country where the prisons are located. If prisons were in major cities, on college campuses, it would be far easier to employ competent staff—clerical, guards, cooks, administrative, and others. Also, the location of a prison on a college campus would provide a greater stimulus for people to seek employment in this field because, then, employment in the prison would have a different and enhanced respectability and desirability.

6. It would convey to the prisoner that he has a respectability; the world is not fearful of him nor have they forgotten him. Rather, his society cares and is interested in him. Through conveying this to prisoners with a failure identity, we could begin to eliminate the emotional problems caused by confinement in a prison facility. For inmates to know that they have not been forgotten or banished is supportive in itself. It would convey to the public also that an understanding and resolution of correctional problems is essential.

7. Part of a rehabilitation program includes visits from people who care about the inmates. The unreasonable locations of most prisons makes accessibility extremely difficult for visitors. If the prison were located in a major city where transportation was convenient and reasonable, we believe that the prisoners would have a greater number of visits from those individuals who are concerned about them, whether they be families, spouses, or friends. This is an integral part of any rehabilitative plan.

8. Although we have acknowledged that the placement of a prison on a college campus would enhance the education of the public and the students in related fields attending that campus, it would also provide an opportunity to educate the prisoners. We propose that a pre-parole program could be outlined and prisoners could be permitted to take courses on the college campus after they had attained a certain stage of rehabilitation and trust. They could continue for a period of time living in the prison and returning to the prison after classes. This of course would not be applicable to every prisoner but could be an incentive and an integral part of the rehabilitative program.

9. Rehabilitative programs in the prisons are totally inadequate partially because the facilities for rehabilitation are located far from the prison facility. On a college campus the opportunity for a rehabilitative program including occupational therapy, recreational therapy, music therapy, library facilities, athletic facilities, and others would be convenient and could be utilized by the correctional facility.

The initiation of a pilot program in this area requires, of course, federal and state approval. We believe that this idea merits at least a pilot program of one or two prisons on one or two college campuses. We believe that it has advantages for the correctional system and for society as a whole.

We cannot belabor our errors in the past; we must begin with the present and look toward the future. Dr. Allen Wheelis expressed this poignantly in his book *The Dessert*.

> Conflict, suffering, psychotherapy—all these lead us to look again at ourselves, to look more carefully, in greater detail, to find what we have missed, to understand a mystery; and all this extends awareness. But whether this greater awareness will increase or diminish freedom will depend on what it is that we become aware of. If the greater awareness is of the causes, traumas, psychodynamics that 'made' us what we are, then we are understanding the past in such a way as to prove that we 'had' to become what we are; and, since this view applies equally to the present which is the unbroken extension of that determined past, therapy becomes a way of establishing why we must continue to be what we have been, a way of disavowing choice with the apparent blessing of science, and the net effect will be a decrease in freedom. If, however, the greater awareness is of options unnoticed, of choices denied, of other ways to live, then freedom will be increased, and with it greater responsibility for what we have been, are, and will become.

# INDEX